PANZERGRENADIER

OSPREY
PUBLISHING

PANZERGRENADIER

Thomas Anderson

OSPREY PUBLISHING
Bloomsbury Publishing Plc
Kemp House, Chawley Park, Cumnor Hill, Oxford OX2 9PH, UK
29 Earlsfort Terrace, Dublin 2, Ireland
1385 Broadway, 5th Floor, New York, NY 10018, USA
E-mail: info@ospreypublishing.com
www.ospreypublishing.com

OSPREY is a trademark of Osprey Publishing Ltd

First published in Great Britain in 2021

ISBN: HB 9781472841797;
eBook 9781472841803;
ePDF 9781472841773;
XML 9781472841780

21 22 23 24 25   10 9 8 7 6 5 4 3 2 1

Conceived and edited by Jasper Spencer-Smith.
Design and artwork: Nigel Pell.
Index: Michael Napier.
Produced by Editworks Limited, Bournemouth BH1 4RT, UK
Originated by PDQ Digital Media Solutions, Bungay, UK
Printed and bound in India by Replika Press Private Ltd.

Osprey Publishing supports the Woodland Trust,
the UK's leading woodland conservation charity.

To find out more about our authors and books visit
www.ospreypublishing.com. Here you will find extracts,
author interviews, details of forthcoming events and
the option to sign up for our newsletter.

CONTENTS

INTRODUCTION

The rapid movement or transfer of larger military formations (infantry) has always been a major problem in warfare, since the marching speed of an equipped infantryman averaged some 4kph. This made it extremely difficult to make a quick and decisive intervention when threatened with invasion. The situation was somewhat alleviated as railway routes began to be built.

By 1936, the first half-tracked self-propelled gun had been designed by Rheinmetall. It was armed with a 3.7cm FlaK 43/1 L/70 gun, mounted in a small open turret, and built using the chassis of a Hansa-Loyd HLkl 3. A short time later, Büssing-NAG produced a similar type of vehicle on their BNL6 chassis, but it was more heavily armed with a 7.5cm L/40.8 gun. Both types were intended to operate in the tank destroyer role; the Bussing-Nag type would have been a formidable light field gun to provide supporting fire. Finally, Hanomag developed a reconnaissance vehicle based on their H 8(H) chassis. None of the three types progressed beyond the prototype stage.

Only at the beginning of the modern era were measures taken to improve mobility. Infantry and *Jäger* (riflemen) were supplied with horses as mobile units, but still went into battle on foot – a form of combat that the 'dashing' cavalry generally rejected.

As nations developed and became more industrialized, the number of motor manufacturers grew and military forces could be equipped with various types of vehicle.

During World War I, Great Britain led the development of the tank and was the first to deploy the type in a battle. These armoured vehicles, fitted with continuous linked track, were intended for use as breakthrough weapons able to negotiate rough terrain, breach trench systems and attack fortified positions. The first to be built were fabricated from an early form of armour plate which

This *Oberfeldwebel* commanding an SdKfz 251 is wearing headphones and a throat-type microphone connected to a *Funksprech* (FuSprech – transceiver) 'd'. The senior NCO has been awarded an *Eisernes Kreuz 1st Klasse* (Iron Cross: First Class) and a *Sportabzeichen* (sports badge).

gave some protection against infantry fire. The tank had a formidable armament: four hull-mounted machine guns and two artillery guns in side sponsons, but conditions inside the vehicle during battle must have been horrendous for the crew.

The tank gave the Allies tactical superiority which, depending on the extent of the attack and the number of vehicles available, would often lead to local or significantly larger territorial gains.

Although this could be seen as an important achievement, the tanks were often isolated behind the frontline and vulnerable to attack. In this dangerous situation, German forces were able to regroup and take advantage of the lack of fire from enemy artillery (and supporting infantry) which allowed their infantry to attack those tanks that had broken through with grenades and explosive charges.

In many instances, expensively captured territory was soon retaken by German forces. Any abandoned tanks would be recovered and taken to workshops where many would be repaired and used against British forces.

In *Reichswehr* service: a 1935 BMW R12, *Beiwagen-Krader* (motorcycle and sidecar [combination]) of a *Kradschützen* unit serves to carry a MG team. A water-cooled 7.92mm *Maschinengewehr* (MG – machine gun) 08, and tripod mounting is carried on the sidecar.

Great Britain reacted and developed the Mk IX Tank, known as the 'Pig', as an armoured infantry carrier that could carry up to 20 men. The hull was fitted with rifle ports on each side to allow them to fire from inside the vehicle. In 1917, an order was issued for 200 vehicles, but only three had been delivered by the end of the war in November 1918. Although the type had many supporters, the Mk IX was cancelled.

Despite the undeniable success achieved by the first tank units, they were unable to turn the World War I into a war of movement. After the war, while Germany faced the severe restrictions enforced by the Treaty of Versailles, the victorious nations concentrated on building up their tank forces.

On 16 March 1935, the *Wehrmacht* (previously the *Reichswehr*) was formed and Germany regained sovereignty over its military. Military planners decided to use the limited resources available to develop and produce tanks.

The majority of the German infantry belonged to the conventional army, but Heinz Guderian realized that his highly mobile Panzers would need an infantry that was capable of closely following an attack. Consequently, he planned for his divisions to include infantry; *Schützen* (riflemen), and it was from these rifle units that a new force emerged in 1942; the *Panzergrenadier* (PzGren – armoured infantry).

The SdKfz 251, later called *mittlerer Schützenpanzerwagen* (m SPW – medium armoured personnel carrier) was based on the chassis of the SdKfz 11. Armed with two *Maschinengewehr* (MG – machine gun) 34, it became the standard combat vehicle for all rifle units.

1

1936 – A NEW INFANTRY

Despite the small number of successful tank operations in World War I, it is a fact that this new weapon had helped break the disastrous stalemate on the Western Front. After the war a study was conducted among the combatants, examining their tactics and strategic policies, by a number of military theorists and historians. One who took an interesting overview was Major-General John F.C. Fuller; he had served in World War I and had at an early stage been involved in planning the tank operation for the Battle of Cambrai in November 1917. Also, he had been with the British tank units during the attack.

In his view the machine gun, although an exceptionally effective means of defence, was easily neutralized by the firepower and armoured protection of a tank. Fuller expounded on his theory in his dissertation, 'The Constant Tactical Factor', in which he stated that in future every new weapon or battle tactic would inevitably be neutralized by a quickly initiated countermeasure. He anticipated further development of the weapons designed, produced and deployed in World War I – artillery, machine guns, tanks, aircraft and chemicals (gas) – as an inevitability:

> Accepting that the main factor in future warfare will be the replacing of manpower by machine power, the logical deduction is that an ideal army to aim for is one man, not a conscripted nation - not even a super scientist - but one man who can press a button or pull a lever and put into operation war machines evolved by the best brains of the nation during peacetime. In the mechanical wars of the future, we must first recognize the fact that the earth is a solid 'sea' and easily traversable in all directions by a tractor - just as a sheet of ice is by a skater. Therefore, the land battles in these wars will more and more be likened to naval actions.

By 1944, the *Schützenpanzerwagen* (SPW – armoured infantry carrier) – here a *Sonderkraftfahrzeug* (SdKfz – special purpose vehicle) 251 – was considered to be essential for all combat operations by PzGren. Many variants were built of both the SdKfz 250 and SdKfz 251. Here the commanding officer of an SdKfz 251/3 *Funkpanzerwagen* (armoured radio vehicle) receives directions from a PzGren during the Battle of the Bulge; 16 December 1944 to 25 January 1945.

Motorcycles, which were not banned under the Treaty of Versailles, became popular as an inexpensive means of transport for the German population. Large numbers were being produced by a variety of manufacturers. Subsequently a significant number were used by the *Reichswehr*, and more so by the *Wehrmacht* after 1935.

If the enemy will not accept peace terms forthwith, then wars in the air and on land will take place between machines to gain superiority. Tank will meet tank while in the air, fleets of flying machines will manoeuvre between the defended areas seeking out and attempting to exterminate each other in a similar fashion to an orthodox naval battle. While these small forces of men, representing perhaps 0.5 percent or 1 percent of the entire population, are powerfully equipped and engrossed in a to-the-death fight with their enemy, their respective nations will continue to supply them with the required weaponry. In a future war, as military fighting manpower dwindles must we expect to see military manufacturing manpower increase.

As an eye witness to those first tank battles and the enormous technical progress, Fuller expected a revolutionary increase in tactical and operational capabilities, and aligned his visions accordingly. As a result, he came to the conclusion that the individual soldier could be supported, if not largely replaced, by the use of modern technology.

His vision did not require individual fighters, battalions, or regiments of foot soldiers. In contrast, the tank, combined in battalions and regiments, was to take over the main burden of fighting in any future wars. In the final analysis he formulated his 'All-Tank' theory, in which he regarded the tank as decisive for war on land, like the battleships of the inter-war period on the high seas.

His ideas, however idealistic, possibly inspired (the then) Major Heinz Guderian and *Oberst* Oswald Lutz as they prepared to assemble the *Panzerwaffe*; an unstoppable mechanized army. Although a total implementation would have been desirable, it was unachievable due to the economic situation and the lack of production facilities in Germany. Also, even the most modern tank was not invincible since it could not operate over all types of terrain.

In 1929, Guderian, recalled in his book, *Erinnerungen eines Soldaten* (A Soldier's Memories):

> In that year I had come to the conclusion that the tank alone, or even in unison with the infantry, could never achieve decisive importance. My own war studies, observation of military exercises in Great Britain and our own forces' manoeuvres using dummy tanks, has strengthened my belief that the tank would only be capable of being truly effective if all the other supporting weapons and units could operate at the same speed and have an adequate off-road capability. The tank force must always lead the attack and all weapons must follow to provide support when requested. Tanks must not be attached

The Krupp-designed and built L2H143 'Protze,' standardized as a *Kraftfahrzeug* (Kfz – motor vehicle) 70, was first produced as a *Mannschaftskraftwagen* (MannschKw – personnel carrier). The vehicle, which carried a driver and seven infantrymen, was also used to tow the 3.7cm *Panzerabwehrkanone* (PaK – anti-tank gun) or a 2cm *Flugzeugabwehrkanone* (FlaK – anti-aircraft gun).

Right: A Stöwer-built *Kraftfahrzeug* (Kfz – motor vehicle) 4, *leichte Einheits Personenkraftwagen* (le EinheitsPkw – light personnel vehicle) fitted with a *Zwillingssockel-Lafette* (ZiSoLa – twin mounting) for two *Maschinengewehr* (MG – machine gun) 34 as a *Truppenluftschutz-Kraftwagen* (TrpLSchKw – anti-aircraft vehicle).

to an infantry division. It is essential for a tank division to be assembled with all the weapons and units needed to be an effective battle force.

In the following years Guderian continued to do everything possible to create an effective force of Panzer divisions, supported by integrated infantry, artillery, field engineers and reconnaissance units. The force would also have *motorisierte* (mot – motorized) supply and replenishment columns. Most importantly, the division would be equipped with reliable voice and Morse radio communications. In his view, only these almost self-contained armoured units would be capable of operating independently, particularly when pursuing retreating enemy forces and then holding the territory gained. It was obvious that the supporting units had to be as fast and mobile as the tanks.

As the German economy recovered and the motor industry began producing all types of vehicle, the *Reichswehr* began to become more mechanized. In the 1920s, the *Inspektion der Kraftfahrtruppen* (inspection of the motorized units) was established, and became responsible for organization, training, materials and replacement equipment.

Above: A photograph taken during one of the first *Versuchsübungen* (trial exercises) for the deployment of a Panzer division. Here a Krupp Kfz 70 MannschKw, carrying *Schützen* (riflemen), passes through a column of PzKpfw I light tanks. (Atlantic/Ullstein via Getty)

The pre-war designed all-wheel-drive, *Einheitsdiesel* (universal diesel) was possibly the most powerful vehicle in German service. It had a cargo capacity of 2,540kg and was classified as a *leichter geländegängiger Lastkraftwagen* (le gl Lkw – light cross-country truck). The type was produced by a number of manufacturers, including Henschel, Magirus and MAN, but it was complicated and expensive to build and was withdrawn from production.

In 1937, regulations were published concerning the responsibilities of the various *Waffengattungen* (service arms):

The Kraftfahrtruppen (motorized units) include:
a) Schützeneinheiten (motorized rifle units)
b) Auflärungseinheiten (motorized reconnaissance units)
c) Panzertruppe (tank units)

In accordance with instructions, *Oberkommando des Heeres* [OKH – Army High Command] will from 25 November 1936 to 18 October 1937 take over the care of the following departments:

a) Schützeneinheiten: Inspektion der Infanterie (Insp 2)
b) Schützeneinheiten: Kavallerie-Abteilung (Insp 3)
c) Panzertruppe: Inspektion der Panzertruppen and for the motorization of the army (Insp 6)

A 7.92mm *Maschinengewehr* (MG – machine gun) 13 mounted on a BMW-built *Beiwagen-Krader* (motorcycle combination). From 1936, the weapon began to be replaced in service by the MG 34.

The distribution of tasks still reflected the traditional views of World War I. Attaching reconnaissance units in their entirety to the cavalry was quite normal by 1930s standards, but this part of the army was to remain independent for the present.

The *Schützeneinheiten* (rifle units) in turn were subject to the inspection of the infantry, since these units were not only to be attached to the InfDiv (mot), but also to the tank divisions. But being under the control of the armoured forces (Insp 6) would have been more logical.

It seems that this logic should eventually prevail. In 1938 the *Kraftfahrtruppen* (motorized forces) were finally replaced by the *Schnellen-Truppen* (rapid forces). This section of the army now included:

Schützeneinheiten (rifle units)
Panzertruppen (armoured units)
Panzerjäger (tank destroyers)
Aufklärung (reconnaissance units)
Reiterei (cavalry)
Ersatztruppen (replacement units)
Waffenschulen (ordnance schools)

Further changes would follow as the war progressed. In 1943, the newly formed *Panzertruppen* replaced the *Schnellen-Truppen*.

2

THE *SCHÜTZENPANZERWAGEN*

In the early 1930s, the *Reichswehr* had only a few World War I-type armoured cars available for training exercises. To overcome this, tanks were replicated by fabricating a dummy superstructure which fitted over the bodywork of a passenger car; some over a bicycle-type frame. Despite being inadequately equipped, Guderian and Lutz worked stubbornly to implement their ideas.

Their vision of a Panzer division (PzDiv – armoured division) was not just a gathering of tanks as represented by an *Abteilung* (Abt – battalion) or *Regimenter* (Rgt – regiment), since units at this level had no supporting weapons, and were generally part of a larger organizational unit. Even the Panzer brigade (PzBrig – armoured brigade) of 1935 had an establishment of two PzRgt each with two PzAbt and both were supplied with signals resources. But reconnaissance operations were the responsibility of a sole *Krad-Schützen-Kompanie* (KradSchtzKp – motorcycle rifle company).

After the war, Guderian wrote in his memoir:

> The development of tracked vehicles as the support weapon of the tanks never took place with the required haste. It was obvious that our tanks would be faster than rifle, artillery and the other units in the division when advancing over difficult terrain. Consequently, we demanded that half-track vehicles with light armour be supplied for the rifle units.

Eventually his opinion was recognized and adopted for the first experimental Panzer division which was established, as follows, in 1934–35:

A Panzer brigade with two regiments; each having two battalions.
A *Schützenbrigade* (SchtzBrig – rifle brigade) one rifle regiment and a

Two SdKfz 251 *ungepanzerte* (ungep – un-armoured) on a forest track carry the marking OAL (*Offiziersanwärter-Lehrgang*) which indicates that they are in service with an officer training unit. The instructors wear a white band around their *Schiffchen* (forage cap).

The first *Mannschaftskraftwagen* (MannschKw – personnel carrier) Kfz 70 used the standardized chassis of the *schwerer Personenkraftwagen* (s Pkw – heavy passenger car). Although it was a reliable design, the type was mechanically too complex for battlefield conditions.

motorcycle rifle battalion
Support units

In August 1935, the first major exercise involving a Panzer division was carried out at the Munster military training area, with the intention of putting theory into practice by trialling the tactics, organization, armament and equipment of this new revolutionary type of unit. After the trials an experience report was produced which confirmed a number of fundamental certainties:

> The tank brigade and rifle brigade of a Panzer division form a community which guarantees success through constant cooperation and mutual support. While the tanks conquer, the riflemen tidy up and hold on to what the tanks have won. Tank units without rifle units and rifle units without tank units hardly seem to be suitable for independent deployment. Their permanent cooperation enables them to be very versatile when in combat.
>
> As soon as enemy fire allows – and before the enemy can form new defensive lines – the closely supporting rifle units must therefore be brought forward to mop up any

remaining pockets of resistance, then widen the front and secure the flanks and make the area safe for our supporting combat vehicles, including tanks preparing for a second phase. The riflemen, as long as the situation permits, should be carried in vehicles and be in close contact with the tanks. [An indication as to the requirement for

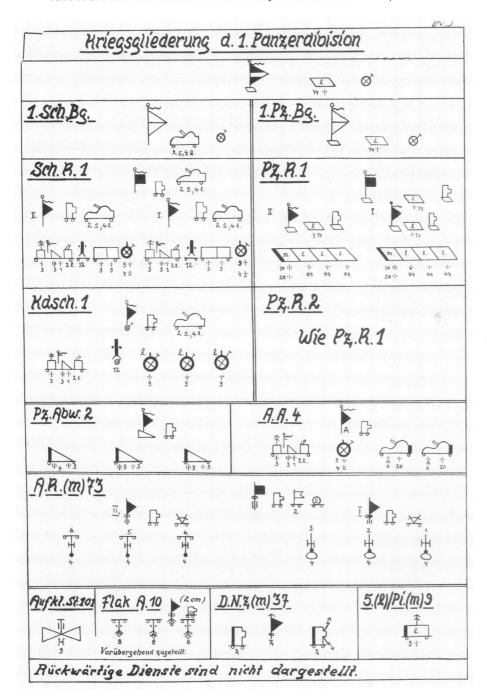

This early structure of 1.PzDiv shows the clear demarcation between *Schützen-Brigade* (SchtzBrig – rifle brigade) and PzBrig. The brigade initially consisted of a rifle regiment and a *Kradschützen-Bataillon* (motorcycle rifle battalion).

Right: After the outbreak of war, the MannschKw was superseded by newer and more simply designed vehicles. This Steyr 1500 had rigid axles instead of mechanically complex independent suspension.

Below: A Krupp Protze (Kfz 70) painted in the pre-1939 *Buntfarben-Anstrich* (multi-colour scheme) camouflage scheme of sand yellow, brown and green. Only the rear four wheels were driven, reducing cross-country mobility.

Above: The *schwerer geländegängiger Personenkraftwagen* (s gl Pkw – heavy cross-country vehicle) was built by Horch and also (German) Ford. The vehicle, which remained in production until 1942, was significantly lower than a Steyr 1500.

Left: The Mercedes-Benz Typ 1500A heavy passenger car remained in production until 1944, after an estimated 5,000 had been delivered. The vehicle had all-wheel drive.

lightly armoured vehicles for rifle units.] If, as the advance moves forward, the enemy makes a localized counterattack, the nearest rifle unit will dismount and attack – possibly assisted by tanks in the support wave – neutralizing the enemy and allowing the advance to continue.

It is essential for a rifle brigade to keep as close contact as safety allows with the Panzer brigade. That is unless, in special circumstances, armoured units have originally been designated to provide protection.

In a battle, if the rifle brigade and the other support units are ordered to secure an area of difficult terrain (including dense woodland) to prevent the Panzer brigade being attacked by enemy mechanized forces, they must be deployed in force and concentrated at a carefully predetermined point on the battlefront. It may often be advisable to use the superior speed of the rifle units to take possession of important points, such as a river crossings, before the Panzer brigade can approach.

Many nations, including Austria, experimented with wheel-cum-track designs. The Austro-Daimler ADMK, had four wheels for driving on firm ground and tracks: the rear wheels were raised for rough terrain.

After evaluation of the first exercises a few changes were introduced before 1.PzDiv was established. Now the theoretical considerations of future equipment had to be defined, realized and implemented.

The motorization of rifle units was achieved by adapting (a cost-effective solution) a number of types of heavy passenger cars and trucks being manufactured by companies in the German motor industry. Due to the large

number of different vehicles available a first attempt at standardization was made, but without success.

The designation *Kraftfahrzeug* (Kfz – motor vehicle) 70, *Mannschaftskraftwagen* (MTW – personnel carrier), was issued for various types produced by a number of manufacturers. Krupp had been producing its L2H43, a 6x4 *leichte geländegängiger Lastkraftwagen* (le gl Lkw – light cross-country vehicle) which carried a driver and seven infantrymen, since 1934. This vehicle was widely used by rifle units and was known, unofficially, as the 'Krupp-Protze'.

Horch designed and built a four-wheel-drive vehicle listed as a *schwere geländegängiger Personenkraftwagen* (s gl Pkw – heavy cross-country passenger car), specifically for military use which carried a driver and six men. The chassis would also be used for the *leichte Panzerspähwagen* (le PzSpWg – light armoured reconnaissance vehicle) and the *Sonderkraftfahrzeug* (SdKfz – special purpose vehicle) 221 to SdKfz 223 series.

The German manufacturer Krauss-Maffei, experimented with the wheel-cum-track concept by fitting a lowerable centre axle on a production KM 10 *Strassenschlepper* (road tractor).

Although originally designed as personnel transports, both vehicles were available with specialized bodies for different applications including a gun tractor, radio car, and an ambulance.

Later in the war, the mechanically complicated and not very reliable Horch-built vehicle was replaced by a simpler, more rugged type of cross-country passenger car manufactured by Mercedes-Benz and the Austrian company Steyr.

These new types of cross-country vehicle performed well on the battlefront. Their simpler engineering made them more economical to produce and they could be delivered in large numbers which allowed an increase in the number of rifle regiments attached to armoured divisions.

However, Guderian continued to demand armoured personnel carriers. Some early statements made by him seem to indicate that he was contemplating the development of a fully combat-capable vehicle for rifle units. Perhaps he had listened to his Panzer commanders and their opinion that the supporting infantry (rifle units) should be capable of fighting from inside their vehicle to take advantage of speed and armour protection to actively intervene in a battle. They would also be capable of undertaking independent combat missions where tanks were not absolutely necessary or available and the riflemen could dismount to attack a specific target.

It is possible that those responsible officers at the *Heereswaffenamt* (HWA – army ordnance office), in the department entrusted with development such types, did not recognize the tactical value of an armed and armoured combat vehicle for the infantry; or did not consider it a feasible project. As in many cases, the solution found was more or less a compromise.

Another, and most likely, reason why the design and development of an armed and fully armoured personnel carrier could not be implemented was the lack of manufacturing capacity in the armaments industry and the prevailing economic situation in Germany. Once again, the HWA was forced to compromise and ordered the development of a vehicle on which, although armoured, the *Panzeraufbau* (armoured body) would have an open top and also a rear door.

The type was designated as a *Mannschaftstransportwagen* (MTW – personnel carrier), indicating that the vehicle was primarily intended for transporting riflemen with the means for them dismount and enter combat as infantry.

After the decision had been made to equip the rifle units in Panzer divisions and also the *leichte Infanterie-Divisionen* (le InfDiv – light infantry divisions) with personnel carriers, a significant number of practical problems arose; military planners had no previous experience of the type which made deployment of the MTW a true challenge.

Moreover, in the mid-1930s priority had been given to the planned mechanization of the Panzer regiments. But the plan had to be postponed, mainly due to the poor economic situation in the Reich, which limited the procurement of vital materials.

The mechanical design of the projected *gepanzerte Mannschaftstransport-wagen* (gep MTW – armoured personnel carrier) was closely linked to the development of the *Zugkraftwagen* (ZgKw – towing vehicle [tractor]) for German artillery units.

Initially, military planners were again faced with a dilemma; *Radfahrzeuge* (wheeled vehicles) represented an economical solution, since many German heavy vehicle manufacturers had sufficient technical experience to adapt production trucks for use by the military. Mechanically most were simple and reliable when operating over paved roads, but mobility was greatly reduced on rough tracks and cross country despite some types being four- or six-wheel-drive vehicles. A number of manufacturers proposed to develop an eight-wheel-drive vehicle, but none materialized and the drive system was only used for a *Panzerspähwagen* (PzSpWg – armoured reconnaissance vehicle).

The *Vollkettenfahrzeuge* (tracked vehicles), on the other hand, had a high degree of mobility even under adverse conditions, such as heavy mud or deep snow, due to their track drive. But there were many disadvantages; they were expensive to produce and required regular and extensive maintenance.

In 1931, Daimler-Benz produced the ZD5 to an order from the Russian Army. Development of the type continued until it entered service with the *Reichswehr* in 1934. The *schwerer Zugkraftwagen* (heavy tractor) designated *Sonderkraftfahrzeug* (SdKfz – special purpose vehicle) 8 was used by the *Wehrmacht* on all battlefronts until 1945.

In the years leading up to the war, German engineers attempted to develop an effective *Selbstfahrlafette* (Sfl – self-propelled) tank destroyer on a half-track chassis; here a Bussing-NAG SdKfz 6. The type was to mount a 7.5cm *Kampfwagenkanone* (KwK – tank gun) L/40.8 (not fitted) in an open turret.

The type also was significantly slower, even on paved roads, than a conventional wheeled vehicle and was also mechanically unreliable.

In the 1930s, a number of hybrid vehicles were developed to combine the advantages of tracked and wheeled vehicles.

The *Räder-Raupen-Fahrzeuge* (wheel-cum-track vehicles) had a fixed track running gear for off-road mobility and usually four lowerable, driven wheels for travelling on surfaced roads. Although a number of nations built experimental wheel-cum-track vehicles, none entered large-scale production, since the type was complex to build and mechanically vulnerable. Importantly, it would have been technically difficult to scale up the mechanics for use on heavy vehicles.

The *Halbketten-Fahrzeug* (half-track vehicle) had advantages similar to those of a wheel-cum-track vehicle, but was easier to build, being much simpler mechanically. During the inter-war years, both France and the German Reich had made significant investments on experimenting with half-track technology. Even before the outbreak of war, France had issued large numbers of halftracks, built by Unic or Somua, to artillery and anti-tank units as gun tractors.

At the same time the German military planners initiated an ambitious project to develop a range of *Zugkraftwagen* (ZgKw – towing vehicle [tractor]):

SdKfz 10: *leichter Zugkraftwagen* 1 ton
SdKfz 11: *leichter Zugkraftwage*n 3 ton

SdKfz 6: *mittlerer Zugkraftwagen* 5 ton
SdKfz 7: *mittlerer Zugkraftwagen* 8 ton
SdKfz 8: *schwerer Zugkraftwagen* 12 ton
SdKfz 9: *schwerer Zugkraftwagen* 18 ton

From 1935, these vehicles were assigned to artillery, tank destroyer, anti-aircraft, repair and recovery units, depending on the tractive power required.

Mechanically, the six basic types had a similar layout: front-mounted engine and gearbox; a non-driven front axle; and tracked running gear. But the type could not be effectively steered by only the front wheels, and an innovative system was adopted: as a turn became tighter a brake would automatically, and progressively, be applied to the inner track.

Many in the military were convinced that a half-track vehicle could not match the high speed of a wheeled vehicle on firm roads, nor the off-road mobility of a fully tracked vehicle. This assessment was undoubtedly correct, but German designers and engineers were able to make considerable improvements to the performance of the type. Those half-track tractors deployed for *Unternehmen* Barbarossa in 1941, proved their value as the advance continued and the terrain changed from dry and dusty to thick wet mud and then deep snow.

At the same time as the type entered service, military planners began to consider if it would be possible to build an armoured personnel carrier on the

The completed prototype of the self-propelled tank destroyer with the 7.5cm KwK L/40.8 mounted. The use of inclined armour plates to form the superstructure later became standard practice on all German armoured half-track vehicles and also armoured cars.

An unknown *Schützen* unit in a garrison holding area. The half-track carriers can be identified as SdKfz 251 Ausf B, which suggests that the photograph was taken shortly before September 1939. All the armoured carriers and the SdKfz 10 are marked with a large Swastika, to identify them to low-flying *Luftwaffe* aircraft.

standard half-track chassis. But the development of German armoured half-track vehicles started differently.

As early as 1935, the *Heereswaffenamt* issued a contract to Rheinmetall-Borsig for them design two types of armoured *Tank-Jäger* (tank destroyer), which were to have superior mobility when compared to a tank.

3.7cm *Selbstfahrlafette* L/70

In 1936, Rheinmetall-Borsig, in cooperation with Hansa-Lloyd, delivered their first armoured *Tank-Jäger* built using components from the HL kl 3 halftrack; a forerunner of the SdKfz 11. The vehicle had a low profile and mounted a 3.7cm PaK L/70 in an open turret. Only one was built.

7.5cm *Selbstfahrlafette* L/40.8

In 1936, Rheinmetall-Borsig received another contract to cooperate with Büssing-NAG in the development of a half-track tank destroyer, mounting a long-barrelled 7.5cm gun. The 7.5cm *Selbstfahrlafette* (Sfl – self-propelled [SP]) L/40.8 – the gun was in some way predecessor of the 7.5cm KwK 40/StuK 40 – had phenomenal firepower for the period. Later in 1936, an upgraded version was commissioned but, possibly due to budgetary constraints, the type did not go into large-scale production.

It seems strange that military planners, at the time, did not give serious consideration to issuing either the 3.7cm PaK L/70 or the 7.5cm KwK L/40.8 for active service with the *Panzerjäger* or the *Panzertruppe*. The 7.5cm gun, especially, would have given both the tank force and anti-tank units a clear superiority in early battles. Unfortunately, an explanation of their decision is impossible due to the lack of contemporary information.

Before the war, the bodywork for a large number of personnel carriers was fabricated from *Weicheisen* (unhardened [mild] steel), which was only proof against long-range infantry fire. Here an SdKfz 251 Ausf B has, for an unknown reason, been armed with a *Maschinengewehr* (MG – machine gun) 13 in place of the standard MG 34.

In winter 1939, German units began an extensive training programme after evaluating combat-experience reports written during the Polish campaign. This unarmoured SdKfz 251/1 carries a 7.92mm MG 34, but without the protective *Panzerschild* (armour shield).

The Armoured Personnel Carrier

There is a small amount of reliable information available on the development of the German armoured personnel carrier; even the original specification documents are not to be found. But it can be assumed with some certainty that Guderian would have had a decisive impact on development by expressing his tactical requirements.

Apparently, military planners had decided on two different vehicles and subsequently issued orders for their development:

A *leichter gepanzerter Mannschaftstransportwagen*, (le gep MTW – light armoured personnel carrier) to transport a *Halbgruppe* (half section: four riflemen) plus the section leader and a driver.

A *mittlerer gepanzerter Mannschaftstransportwagen*, (m gep MTW – medium armoured personnel carrier) to transport a *Gruppe* (a section: ten riflemen) plus the section leader and a driver.

The *Panzeraufbau* (armoured body) on both was fabricated from armour plates angled to deflect 7.92mm *Spitzgeschoss mit Kern* (SmK – armour-piercing ammunition) fire from infantry weapons and shrapnel from artillery fire.

The SdKfz 250

The le gep MTW was designed to carry a section of five riflemen and their equipment. The type was to be built on the chassis of an SdKfz 10, which had to be shortened and modified for the purpose. Demag of Wetter (Ruhr) was responsible for chassis production while six other companies were subcontracted to supply components, including the *Panzeraufbau* (armoured body). Final assembly was carried out by Demag, but as demand for the vehicle increased, Mechanische Werke at Cottbus and Saurer Werke in Vienna were contracted to produce the le gep MTW.

Delivery had been hoped for in 1940, but due to the ever-present shortage of materials and production capacity, it did not enter service until mid-1941. The vehicle was designated *Sonderkraftfahrzeug* (SdKfz – special purpose vehicle) 250.

When the type had been authorized for production, little thought had been given to planning future variants. But a priority order was issued for the production of two specialized types to be built using the same components as those for the forthcoming SdKfz 250. Both entered limited production at the beginning of 1940: the SdKfz 253, *leichter gepanzerter Beobachtungskraftwagen*

Technical Data (basic vehicle):		
	SdKfz 250	**SdKfz 251**
Weight (Empty):	4,600kg	7,000kg
Payload (Crew & Weapons):	1,100kg	1,500kg
Combat Weight:	5,800kg	8,500kg
Engine:	Maybach HL42TUKRM	Maybach HL42TUKRR
Capacity:	4,198cc	4,198cc
Speed (Maximum):	65kph	50kph
Range:	320km	00km
Towing Capacity:	1,000kg	3,000kg
Gradient (Maximum):	240	240
Ground Clearance:	28.5cm	32cm
Trench Crossing:	1.9m	2m
Fording Depth:	70cm	50cm
Radio (Transceiver):	FuSprpGr 'a'	FuSprGr 'a'

The SdKfz 251 had the same towing capacity as the SdKfz 11, which made it suitable for towing the 3.7cm *Panzerabwehrkanone* (PaK – anti-tank gun) or the 7.5cm *leichter Infanteriegeschütz* (le IG – light infantry gun) 18.

(le gep BeobKw – light armoured observation vehicle) and the SdKfz 252, *leichter gepanzerter Munitionskraftwagen* (le gep MunKw – light armoured ammunition carrier), both were initially issued in small numbers to the newly formed *Sturmartillerie* (StuArt – assault artillery) units: *Sturmgeschütz-Batterien* (StuGBttr – assault gun batteries) and later *Sturmgeschütz-Abteilungen* (StuGAbt – assault gun battalions).

Deliveries of the SdKfz 250 for the rifle units was scheduled to begin by mid-1941. A *Waffenamt* document, dated November 1940, lists the following planned variants:

SdKfz 250: the basic *leichter gepanzerter Zugkraftwagen* (le gep ZgKw – light armoured towing vehicle).

SdKfz 250/1: *leichter Schützenpanzerwagen als Zugführerfahrzeug* (le SPW – platoon leader's vehicle); *le Maschinengewehr Trupp* (le MG Trp – light machine gun section); *Zugfahrzeug für PaK* (anti-tank gun tractor).

SdKfz 250/2: *leichter Fernsprech-Panzerwagen* (le FernSpr PzWg – light telephone cable vehicle).

SdKfz 250/3: *leichter Funk-Panzerwagen* (le Fu PzWg – light armoured radio vehicle).

SdKfz 250/4: *leichter Truppenluftschutz-Panzerwagen* (le TrpLSchtz PzWg – light anti-aircraft vehicle).

SdKfz 250/5: *leichter Beobachtungs-Panzerwagen für Sturmartillerie* (le BeobPzWg – light observation vehicle for assault gun artillery).

SdKfz 250/6: *leichter Munitions-Panzerwagen für Sturmartillerie* (le MunPzWg – light ammunition vehicle for assault artillery).

The list shows that the SdKfz 252 and SdKfz 253 in service with the *Sturmartillerie* were to be replaced by the SdKfz 250/5 and SdKfz 250/6 variants.

The SdKfz 251

Design and development of this large (although designated as a medium) armoured personnel carrier had been initiated long before the outbreak of war. The vehicle used the chassis of the SdKfz 11 half-track tractor on which, unlike the SdKfz 10, the suspension was mounted on a subframe, protected by an additional armour belly plate.

The type was designated *Sonderkraftfahrzeug* (SdKfz – special purpose vehicle) 251 and by the end of the war some 15,252, including all variants (22), had been assembled by Hanomag, Adlerwerke, Horch (Auto-Union), Škoda and Borgward.

Production

At the beginning of 1939, officials in the *Heereswaffenamt* (HWA) were aware of the urgent requirement for an armoured personnel carrier and issued an order for 1,000 vehicles with production to begin immediately. But German steel manufacturers were working to capacity, which meant it would be impossible to meet this target. Consequently, a decision was taken to produce part of the order with an 'armoured' body fabricated from mild steel and a total of 305 were completed as *ungepanzerte* (ungep – unarmoured) medium personnel carriers: 232 were completed as *gepanzerte* (gep – armoured). Both types were designated as SdKfz 251 since they would be deployed for the same purpose on the battlefront.

The unarmoured vehicles were fabricated from 4mm mild steel sheet, which prevented the crew compartment from being penetrated by 7.92mm infantry ammunition from a range of over 30m. However, the body of the armoured version was fabricated from 8mm plating (14.5mm at the front) which gave protection from 7.92mm *Spitzgeschoss mit Kern* (SmK – armour-piercing ammunition), but again from a range of over 30m.

A ten-man *Schützengruppe* (rifle squad) in an SdKfz 251/1 during a training exercise. The standard weapon has been replaced by a *schwere Maschinengewehr Lafette* (s MG – heavy machine-gun carriage) 34 fitted with a *Zielfernrohr* (Zf – periscopic sight) so that it could be fired from inside the vehicle.

To allow the manufacturers to concentrate on producing the large numbers required, the completed *Grundfahrzeuge* (basic vehicles) would be delivered directly from the works to *Heereszeugamt* (HZA – army depots) where each would be fitted with the equipment – radios and weaponry – specified for the individual variant (see below). Special fittings, such as *Zusatzhalter* (additional holders), had to be requisitioned from the army depot responsible for the distribution of such items.

The vehicles were then delivered to a unit and distributed – not always exactly – in accordance to the respective current *Kriegsstärkenachweisung* (KStN – table of organization).

Variants

German military planners envisaged a number of specialized variants for various tactical applications. In November 1940, a list of these was published for the first time in an *Allgemeinen Heeresmitteilungen* (general army bulletin), but the list was to be adapted and modified as the war progressed. It was also noted in the bulletin that the original designation *Mannschaftstransportwagen* (MTW) was to be replaced by *Schützenpanzerwagen* (SPW).

[Note: both *Mannschaftstransportwagen* and *Schützenpanzerwagen* continued to be used until the end of the war. Sometimes it was also referred to as the *Panzergrenadierwagen* (PGW – armoured riflemen vehicle.]

SdKfz 251 as the basic form for all applications (*mittlerer gepanzerter Zugkraftwagen* (m gep ZgKw – medium armoured towing vehicle).

The SdKfz 251/1 Ausf A carried a tarpaulin specially made to fit over the crew compartment to protect the interior and equipment against bad weather.

Two of the SdKfz 251/1 Ausf B, identifiable by the reduced number of vision apertures in the side of the superstructure. The vehicles are among those in the image on page 30.

SdKfz 251/1: *für Schützen- und schwere Maschinengewehr Gruppe* (SPW u s MG – rifle and heavy machine gun section).

SdKfz 251/2: *für leichte und schwere Granatwerfer* (SPW GrW – for light and heavy grenade launcher [mortar]).

SdKfz 251/3: *für Infanteriegeschütz* (SPW [IG] – light infantry gun).

SdKfz 251/4: *für Infanteriegeschütz*: Munition (SPW [IG: Mun] – ammunition carrier for light infantry gun).

SdKfz 251/5: *für Pionier-Züge der Schützeneinheiten* (SPW [Pi] – for pioneer platoons in rifle units).

SdKfz 251/6: *mittlerer Kommando-Panzerwagen als Führerfahrzeug mit Funkeinbauten* (m KdoPzWg – medium command vehicle with radio).

SdKfz 251/7: *mittlerer Pionier-Panzerwagen für Panzerpionier-Bataillon* (m PiPzWg – medium armoured vehicle for the engineer battalion)

SdKfz 251/8: *mittlerer Kranken-Panzerwagen für Krankentransport* (m KrPzWg – medium armoured ambulance).

3

1939 – POLAND

In 1939, the Panzer divisions still presented a very uneven picture in terms of the rifle elements, organization and equipment. The first three Panzer divisions – 1.PzDiv, 2.PzDiv and 3.PzDiv – established in 1935, received an effective infantry element consisting of a *Schützen-Brigade* (SchtzBrig – rifle brigade) in addition to a Panzer brigade. This was assembled as a regiment of two battalions and an independent motorcycle rifle battalion. A few years later, in 1939, another two Panzer divisions were formed; 4.PzDiv was identical to the first three, whereas 5.PzDiv was supplied with a *Schützen-Brigade* of two regiments, each of which had two rifle battalions but no independent motorcycle rifle battalion.

When 10.PzDiv was ready for battle in the months before the outbreak of war, the unit initially had only a conventional infantry regiment (mot); this sub-unit had been taken over by the 29.InfDiv.

The main body of the *Schützen-Bataillon* (SchtzBtl – rifle battalion) in a pre-war Panzer division, organized to the relevant *Kriegstärkenachweisung* (KStN – table of organization), was to have the following elements (staff and supply services not included):

Schützen-Kompanie 'b' (*motorisiert*) (SchtzKp [mot] – rifle company [motorized], to KStN 1114.
Maschinengewehr-Kompanie 'b' (mot) (MGKp – machine-gun company [motorized]), to KStN 1116.
Krad-Schützen-Kompanie (KradSchtzKp – motorcycle rifle company), to KStN 1111.
Krad-Maschinengewehr-Kompanie (KradMGKp – motorcycle machine-gun company), to KStN 1118.

The Kfz 4 *Truppenluft-schutzKraftwagen* was fitted with two MG 34 in a *Zwillingsockel-Lafette* (ZiSoLa - twin mounting). The carrier vehicle, a *leichter geländegäniger Personenkraftwagen* (le gl Pkw - light cross-country personnel vehicle) was built by Stöwer and had four-wheel drive and steering.

Heavy Company

Panzerabwehrkanone-Zug (PzAbwehr-Zug – anti-tank gun platoon): three 3.7cm PaK, to KStN 1222.

Infanteriegeschütz-Zug (*motorisiert*) (IG Zg [mot] – infantry gun platoon [motorized]): two 7.5cm *leichte Infanteriegeschütz* (le IG – light infantry gun) 18, to KStN 1123.

Pionier-Zug (PiZg – engineer platoon), to KStN 1124.

(Note: individual strengths cannot be described in detail and a comparison of the fighting strengths is not very useful.)

An example Schützen-Brigade 1 of 1.PzDiv (September 1939) is shown in the following table.

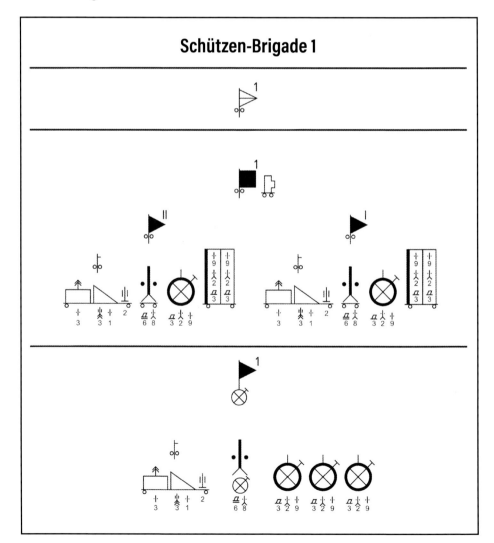

The organizational structure of Schützen-Brigade 1 shows that it had two rifle battalions and a motorcycle rifle battalion.

When the first Panzer divisions were established, the rifle companies were initially equipped with conventional wheeled vehicles, designated *Kraftfahrzeug* (Kfz – motor vehicle) 70 for transporting personnel.

When production of the light and medium armoured personnel carrier (SdKfz 251 and the later 250) began, it was initially planned to issue these vehicles to rifle units. The valid KStNs were respectively rewritten

Schützen-Kompanie b (KStN 1114)							
Kp Trupp	1. Zug	2. Zug	3. Zug	s MG Halbzug	Gefechts-Tross	Gepäck-Tross	Hilfs-Trupp
Kfz 15	Kfz 70	Kfz 70	Kfz 70	Kfz 15	Kfz 15		
Kfz 15						le gl Lkw	le gl Lkw
	Kfz 70	Kfz 70	Kfz 70	Kfz 70	le gl Lkw		
	Kfz 70	Kfz 70	Kfz 70	Kfz 70	le gl Lkw		
	Kfz 70	Kfz 70	Kfz 70		le gl Lkw		
	Kfz 70	Kfz 70	Kfz 70		le gl Lkw		
	Kfz 70	Kfz 70	Kfz 70				
	Kfz 70	Kfz 70	Kfz 70				

A standard motorized *Schützen-Kompanie* (Schtz-Kp – rifle company) was issued with Kfz 70 heavy passenger cars.

In 1939, many of the non-mechanized infantry divisions relied on the horse for their main means of transport, even the divisional artillery. Some 2,750,000 horses were procured by the German army during World War II and were used to haul everything from a *Feldküche* (field kitchen) to a heavy artillery gun.

(the *Kradschützen* units remained unchanged) and the acronym 'gp' – for *gepanzert* (armoured) – was used to indicate those that should be equipped with the armoured personnel carrier:

Schützen-Kompanie 'b' (gp), to KStN 1114(gp)
Maschinengewehr-Kompanie 'b' (gp), to KStN 1116(gp)
Schwere Kompanie (heavy company):
Panzer-Abwehr-Zug (gp): three 3.7cm PaK, to KStN 1222(gp)
Infanteriegeschütz-Zug (gp): two 7.5cm le IG 18, to KStN 1123(gp)
Pionier-Zug (gp), to KStN 1124(gp)

Military planners intended to include both light and medium armoured personnel carriers into the sub-units depending on the number of troops and equipment to be carried. The decision to build the SdKfz 250 was made in 1939, but due to manufacturing problems – mainly insufficient capacity – it did not enter service until mid-1941. As a consequence, the order issued for the SdKfz 250 was to be substituted by the SdKfz 10/1, half-track tractor.

As the production of the SdKfz 251 was also affected by bottlenecks in the production of armour steel, a considerable number of unarmoured personnel carriers were built, which are difficult to recognize externally. They were used to substitute the missing armoured SdKfz 251 in the rifle units.

A total of 94 (unarmoured) and 68 SdKfz 251/2 (armoured) had been manufactured by the end of August 1939 and an order was issued for the majority [the numbers are unknown] to be delivered to Schützen-Regiment (SchtzRgt – rifle regiment) 1. As a result, 1.PzDiv received a number of these valuable vehicles immediately before the start of *Fall Weiss* (Case White), the invasion of Poland on 1 September 1939. It is not known how many armoured personnel carriers were delivered to other tank divisions before the invasion, but it is possible that a small number were issued to test the type under battlefield conditions.

Due to the late delivery of equipment it was hardly possible to train the riflemen on their new weapon system; the first combat operations using the type resembled a poorly organized troop trial.

Schützen-Kompanie b (gp) (KStN 1114)
SchtzRgt 1, 1.PzDiv as of September 1939

Kp Trupp	1. Zug	2. Zug	3. Zug	s MG Halbzug	Gefechts-Tross	Gepäck-Tross	Hilfs-Trupp
SdKfz 10	SdKfz 251	SdKfz 251	SdKfz 251	SdKfz 10	Kfz 15		
SdKfz 251						le gl Lkw	le gl Lkw
	SdKfz 251	SdKfz 251	SdKfz 251	SdKfz 251	le gl Lkw		
	SdKfz 251	SdKfz 251	SdKfz 251	SdKfz 251	le gl Lkw		
	SdKfz 251	SdKfz 251	SdKfz 251		le gl Lkw		
					le gl Lkw		

A new organizational structure was produced for the introduction of armoured personnel carriers.

The *mittlerer geländegängiger Personenkraftwagen* (m gl Pkw - medium cross-country personnel vehicle) was built in many versions by a number of manufacturers. The Kfz 12 could carry up to five men and had a towing capacity of some 1,000kg, which meant the type could haul light anti-tank and infantry guns.

Rifle Units in Light Divisions

In 1938, four *leichte Divisionen* (le Div – light divisions) were formed from cavalry units and were also part of the *schnellen Truppen* (rapid forces) – later *Panzertruppen*. The 1.le Div was assigned a *Kavallerie-Schützen-Regiment* (KavSchtzRgt – cavalry rifle regiment) formed of three rifle battalions and a motorcycle rifle battalion. Conversely, 2.le Div, 3.le Div and 4.le Div received two KavSchtzRgt, each with two rifle battalions.

Due to the short life of the light divisions (all were reformed as regular Panzer divisions immediately after the Polish campaign), the exact organizational structure of these rifle units is not known. It can be assumed that the weaponry of the cavalry rifle companies was almost the same as that of the conventional rifle companies, only the equipment with motor vehicles could differ. Armoured personnel carriers were not assigned. The KStN issued for the formation of the rifle elements would have been identical.

Combat in Poland

The surprising success of the campaign in Poland clearly demonstrated the high combat value of German *motorisiert* (motorized) units. Here the Panzer divisions had a decisive share. Their rifle units also proved their worth, but fought mostly dismounted without direct support. In this campaign the first

experiences of war were gained by this newest branch of the armed forces. These were evaluated after the campaign.

Schützen Elements of Panzer Divisions

The XIX.Armeekorps (AK – Army Corps) fought with Heeresgruppe Nord (Army Group North). On 29 September 1939, the *Generalkommando* (GenKdo – corps headquarters) submitted a report on the experiences in Poland of those *Schützen-Brigaden* (rifle brigades) in 3.PzDiv and 10.PzDiv to the *Oberbefehlshaber des Heeres* (ObdH – commander-in-chief of the army):

> The *Schützen-Regiment* [rifle regiment] must be strengthened to three battalions. The *Kradschützen-Kompanien* [motorcycle rifle companies] within the *Schutzen-Bataillon* [rifle battalion] are indispensable and must be maintained and strengthened. All *Panzer-Aufklärung-Kompanien* [armoured reconnaissance companies] are part of the staff battalions and higher echelons. The armoured personnel carrier is considered to be a vitally important vehicle and production must be accelerated.

Infantry Division (mot)

Before the war, a number of infantry divisions were reorganized as motorized

This Kfz 12 was also used as a staff car for senior officers. The bodywork on this vehicle has been peppered, possibly by shrapnel from an exploding shell, but remains serviceable.

standard infantry divisions (InfDiv [mot]), and issued with significantly more motor vehicles than a normal infantry division.

The *Generalkommando* reported:

> The reconnaissance battalion is too small, it must be restructured similar to those in the tank divisions. The infantry elements of the infantry divisions (mot) are too large, and they lack cross-country mobility. The artillery and signals elements, and the engineer and anti-tank units, proved to be efficient.
>
> The InfDiv (mot) lack tanks and we must consider converting these to Panzer divisions to give them more thrust.

GenKdo of XIX.Armeekorps added some notes on the equipment:

> The effectiveness of the equipment has met my high expectations. Our main concern is replacement parts; the supply of tracks for tanks and rubber pads for half-track tractors and personnel carriers is totally insufficient. If this is not remedied immediately, those affected units are expected to soon become completely immobile. If sufficient spare parts are available within about 14 days, an 80 percent combat readiness can be achieved.

In 1943, all InfDiv (mot) which remained active were to be transferred to the *Panzertruppe* and regrouped as a completely new organization: *Panzergrenadier-Divisionen* (PzGrenDiv – armoured infantry divisions).

Above: A Horch-built m gl Pkw in service as a Kfz 15 *Funkkraftwagen* (FuKw – radio vehicle): note the radio equipment behind the driver.

Far left: A column of SdKfz 251/1, from 1.PzDiv, cross an anti-tank ditch during the initial phase of *Fall Weiss*, 3 September 1939. Only small number of half-track personnel carriers were available at that time; their deployment seems to have been a trial under combat conditions.

Sturm-FlaK (assault anti-aircraft guns) were integral elements in the *Schützen* units. The chassis of an SdKfz 10 was selected to carry the 2cm FlaK 30 (later FlaK 38) gun – which could be dismounted – and designated (respectively) SdKfz 10/4 or SdKfz 10/5. The *Sonderanhänger* (SdAnh – special purpose trailer) 51 normally had a metal box to carry ammunition.

Light Divisions

In 1939, four *leichte Divisionen* (le Di – light divisions) were also available and were planned as armoured units, but with improved tactical mobility. All were equipped with heavy trucks and *Sonderanhänger* (SdAnh – special purpose trailer) 115, so that the armoured elements could be moved quickly over long distances to reduce mechanical wear on the precious tanks.

Due to the fact that they belonged to the *Schnellen-Truppen* (rapid forces), their infantry elements were called *Schützen* (riflemen) and since they were formed from cavalry units, their *Kompanien* (Kp – companies) were designated as *Schwadron* (squadrons).

Compared to standard Panzer divisions, the light divisions had a larger complement of light tanks, resulting in a significantly lower combat strength. This was a tribute to their strategic mobility. However, the advantage of fast and long-range deployment could only be exploited in Western Europe with its good road network. Because of these reasons it had been decided long before the launch of *Fall Weiss* (Case White) to reorganize these units as regular tank divisions.

The following after-action report, dated 8 October 1939, was delivered by the commander of 2.le Div:

Experience during the campaign in Poland

The light division has proven its value during the campaign. Their firepower was sufficient for the tasks set to the division (advance on the river Vistula). Its main advantage over the Panzer divisions equipped with heavier tanks is manoeuvrability and the ability to be transferred over long distances (500km and more).

The PzKpfw I and PzKpfw II are not sufficiently armoured and also lack effective firepower. The front plate on the PzKpfw II is too thin and easily penetrated by the Polish infantry anti-tank rifle at 100m. It is proposed to equip all the light divisions with only the PzKpfw I. Although this tank is more lightly armed, it would be a suitable reconnaissance vehicle for a Panzer division.

Equipping the rifle squad with two machine guns proved to be inappropriate in the attack, since too many infantrymen have to be used as ammunition carriers, resulting in a reduction of rifle fire. During the many firefights in woodland, this problem became apparent not only with motorcycle-mounted riflemen, but also with the rifle squads. It has been proven that every man – except the No.1 and No.2 machine gunners – must be armed with a *Karabiner* [rifle] 98k. The rifle squadron should be equipped with one or two machine guns depending on the mission and the combat situation: a permanent reserve of machine guns and carbines must be available at all times.

A line of *Kradschützen*, mounted on BMW R12 motorcycle combinations, pass elements of an anti-tank unit. The rider is wearing a standard issue long waterproof raincoat.

Above: The sidecar could be fitted with a rigid bar to carry a 7.92mm MG 34 on a special swivel-type mounting. Note the *Metalldauer-Gurt* (reusable metal belt) ammunition.

Right: The sidecar on the majority of heavy motorcycle combinations, here a Zündapp KS750, had a driven wheel which improved mobility. In an emergency, the type had sufficient power to tow a light load, or even a 3.7cm PaK.

Our *Stiel-Handgranate* (stick-type hand grenade) is inferior to the Polish egg-shaped grenade. The stick grenade is too unwieldy, especially when fighting in a wooded area where it can become caught in the branches of a tree, endangering the thrower.

Motorcycle Units

Many after-action reports emphasize the benefits of an independent *Kradschützen-Bataillon* (KradBtl – motorcycle battalion) and a *Kradschützen-Kompanie* (KradKp – motorcycle company) within the rifle units.

During the build-up phase of the *Wehrmacht*, the general level of motorization was low due to a lack of motor manufacturers and subsequently the availability of suitable vehicles: conversely, there were a large number of companies mass-producing motorcycles. German military planners saw the type as a quick and cost-effective way of providing mobility and began procuring significant numbers of light and heavy machines for the newly formed *Wehrmacht*. Subsequently, motorcycle-mounted rifle units were formed for the *Panzerwaffe* and light divisions.

Most types of motorcycle were mechanically reliable, robust and easy to drive, allowing troops a high level of tactical mobility. The more powerful (heavy) types fitted as a *Beiwagen-Kräder* (BeiKrad – motorcycle and sidecar [combination]) could be armed with a machine gun and carried a crew of

German *Pioniere* (Pi – engineers) use a *grosser Flosssack* (large inflatable [dinghy]) to ferry two BMW R12 combinations over a water obstacle. This illustrates one of the benefits of a unit being equipped with light vehicles and also light tactical weapons, such as the 3.7cm PaK.

three – gunner, loader and driver. In combat, the weapon could be fired from the sidecar or quickly dismounted if required.

Initially, the main task of the *Kradschützen* was reconnaissance, but due to their speed, even off road they soon proved capable of accomplishing infantry operations and surprise missions. Although lightly armed, they developed into a remarkable infantry fighting force.

On 30 September 1939, an anonymous KradSchtzBtl delivered an experience report:

An SdKfz 251/1 Ausf A with a spare wheel bolted on the protective plate covering the engine-cooling radiator. Towards end of the invasion of Poland, the conspicuous large white (*Balkenkreuz*) crosses, often used as an aiming point by enemy anti-tank gunners, were altered by painting the centre of each bar *dunkelgrau* (dark grey).

> All motorcycles are overloaded, since in colder weather the crew has to carry sufficient winter clothing and blankets for three. If these items of equipment are carried on the baggage train, they are often not available when needed.
>
> The mounting brackets for the *Maschinengewehr* [MG - machine gun] on the sidecar are still too weak and break with some frequency. The travelling support for the MG is useless, because it cannot be released quickly enough while on the move.
>
> The supporting stays on the sidecar mudguard are too weak and break easily. The tyres are not able to cope with the high stress (weight) and wear out quickly.

A fundamental problem with the BeiKrad was that it only carried a maximum of three, resulting in large numbers being required for a mission.

Kradschützen-Kompanie (KStN 1111)

Kp Trupp	1. Zug	2. Zug	3. Zug	s MG Halbzug	Gefechts-Tross	Gepäck-Tross

The *Kradschützen* (motorcycle rifle) company provided the rifle brigade with considerable firepower.

Tactical Issues

The new type of warfare, which quickly became known as *Blitzkrieg* (lightning war), unleashed against Poland on 1 September 1939, required a number of rapid spearhead attacks to be initiated by armoured forces along a wide battlefront. Although well practiced by German forces during tactical-training exercises, in reality the troops lacked actual combat experience. This same lack not only affected the fighting man, but officers at all levels in command echelons.

The focus of the fighting (and high expectations) was not only on the Panzer divisions, but also on light divisions and the motorized infantry divisions.

Two machine gun teams, armed with the 7.92mm *Maschinengewehr* (MG – machine gun) 34, take up position behind one of the many trees that border a road in the Polish countryside.

On 28 September 1939, *Generaloberst* (*Feldmarschall* in 1943) Ewald von Kleist, commander of XXII.Armeekorps, reported on the fighting in southern Poland:

1.) Leaders to the front.

In the first few days, some leaders of mobile units led from 'command posts' positioned to the rear. If an emergency situation arose at the front, due to enemy resistance, it took too long to transmit any orders from the command post to the troops. Leaders of motorized units and Panzer divisions have to lead from the front, just like cavalry commanders, and

The crew of a SdKfz 10/4, despite lacking any form of protection, fire on enemy infantry holding a fortified position. The 2cm FlaK 30 was a formidable attack or defensive weapon that could fire high-explosive or armour-piercing ammunition.

must personally order their tank troops forward. As a consequence of direct orders from the GenKdo, these commanders took rapid and decisive action.

2.) Protection of the flanks of motorized units.

When the GenKdo took over command on 2 September, the corps was largely flanked by a reconnaissance regiment on the right and a motorcycle battalion on the left. This approach was chosen because Polish counterattacks against the flanks were expected. This cautious approach was also adopted by the divisions. An often over-exaggerated concern for the protection of our flanks, and even rear elements, considerably slowed the pace of our advance.

Motorized units cannot protect their flanks simply by detaching units, due to the speed of the attack. Flanks can only be monitored by air and battlefield reconnaissance; a temporary threat must be accepted. Our troops quickly accepted this action.

3.) Advancing in the face of enemy resistance.

In the first days, the advance of the leading elements of our motorized units were often halted due to the enemy having destroyed bridges and laid mines, and determined resistance by a number of individual units. They only moved forward after this resistance was broken. The GenKdo ordered all units not to fight any pockets of resistance, but to bypass them and continue to advance with the motorized units. Any pocket of resistance was to be attacked and eliminated by supporting units. Consequently, the speed of our advance increased considerably.

The report illustrates how the concept of fast-moving armour and troops, the later *Panzertruppen*, began shaping modern warfare.

The concept of leadership from the front (Item 1) was introduced before the war as a basic doctrine in the *Heer* (army). This was proven in the Polish campaign and later during *Fall Gelb* (Case Yellow), the invasion of The Low Countries and France in 1940, where consistent leadership was shown to be efficient and effective. Both Guderian and Rommel were advocates, as indicated by the many combat successes achieved by the units they commanded.

The concerns raised under Item 2 identified a potential danger. By not protecting the flanks, a tactically skilled opponent could wreak havoc on units forming the spearhead. The danger was eventually recognized during *Unternehmen* (Operation) Barbarossa, the invasion of the Soviet Union.

Item 3, however, was correctly identified. The fast advance deep into enemy territory had to keep moving in order to secure an objective. If the tank assault came to a halt, the advantage would be lost. Here a well-trained, alert unit leader or field commander could quickly react to an unexpected situation and take decisive action.

Two SdKfz 251/1 pause in the ruins of a Polish town. The leading vehicle is fitted with pivot-type mountings (front and rear) for the MG 34. The *Panzerschild* (armour shield) for the front-mounted machine gun began to be fitted in late 1940.

4

1940 — FRANCE

After the successful Poland campaign, the experiences of the individual units should be evaluated. Subsequently, various changes were introduced at the organizational level of the *Schützen-Brigaden* (SchtzBrig – rifle brigades).

At the beginning of September 1939, the *Schützenbrigade* in the first six Panzer divisions (1.PzDiv, 2.PzDiv, 3.PzDiv, 4.PzDiv, 5.PzDiv and 10.PzDiv) was still formed with a total of four *Schützen-Kompanien* (SchtzKp – rifle companies), five *Kradschützen-Kompanien* (KradSchtzKp – motorcycle rifle companies), three *Maschinengewehr-Kompanien* (MGKp – machine-gun companies) and three *schwere Kompanien* (s Kp – heavy companies): *Pionier-Zug* (PioZg – field engineers platoon), *Panzerjäger-Zug* (PzJgZg – anti-tank platoon), *Infanterie-Zug* (InfZg – infantry platoon). As always, minor deviations were the rule.

In October 1939, the four *leichte Divisionen* (le Div – light divisions) were restructured as regular Panzer divisions: 6.PzDiv, 7.PzDiv, 8.PzDiv and 9.PzDiv were established and each was assigned a rifle brigade. The 9.PzDiv was an exception: for unknown reasons the brigade level was not occupied and the two regiments acted independently.

After the fall of Poland, all German units involved were ordered to submit detailed after-action reports of their experiences on the battlefront.

All were collected and collated before being sent for evaluation. Many contained suggestions to improve the 'in the field' organization and command of all formations; from division to regiment and also company level.

The performance of all types of German weaponry, vehicles and the forces involved was also scrutinized in detail.

The General Command of the XIX Army Corps, to which 3.PzDiv was attached, reported on 29 September 1939:

Elements of a Panzer division cross a pontoon bridge over the river Meuse (Maas) near Dinant in the Ardennes region of Belgium. Both vehicles are early SdKfz 251/1 Ausf A halftracks: Note the hatches on the side of the engine cover have been opened to improve ventilation to the engine.

Schützen-Brigade [rifle brigade]:

The *Schützen-Regiment* must be reinforced to three battalions. The *Kradschützen-Abteilung* within the SchtzRgt are indispensable and must be retained or restored. Armoured reconnaissance detachments organically belong to the staffs of the battalions upwards. The manufacture of SdKfz 251 must be urgently accelerated.

In May 1940, after evaluating combat experiences, the composition of the ten Panzer divisions was altered, but not with any consistency:

Organizational Structure	Schtz Brig	Schtz Rgt	Schtz Btl	Schtz Kp	KradScht Btl	KradScht Kp	MG Kp	s Kp
September 1939	1	1	2	4	1	5	3	3
1.PzDiv 1940	1	1	3	7	1	4	4	3
2.PzDiv 1940	1	1	3	7	1	4	4	3
3.PzDiv 1940	1	1	3	7	1	4	4	3
4.PzDiv 1940	1	2	4	11	0	1	2	3
5.PzDiv 1940	1	2	4	8	0	4	0	4
6.PzDiv 1940	1	1	3	9	1	3	4	4
7.PzDiv 1940	1	2	4	12	1	2	0	5
8.PzDiv 1940	1	1	3	9	1	3	4	4
9.PzDiv 1940	0	2	4	12	0	0	0	4
10.PzDiv 1940	1	2	4	11	0	1	4	2

Two SdKfz 251/1 from 3.PzDiv or 4.PzDiv prepare to move out of a French town. The letter 'K', stencilled in white on the lamp cover, indicates that they are attached to Panzergruppe Kleist.

An unknown number of Sdkfz 251 used as command vehicles were fitted with a full-width wooden table which allowed large maps of a battlefront to be examined. The vehicle carries the oak leaf symbol of 1.PzDiv.

Among the many changes in the new PzDiv was an increase in the number of machine guns: the rifle companies now had 18 instead of nine.

Some of the pioneer platoons were removed from the heavy rifle companies and attached to the battalion staffs. For unknown reasons some rifle brigades were not issued with pioneer platoons. Once again, the rifle units presented an extremely uneven picture. Accordingly, the number of heavy weapons assigned to them varied greatly.

Authorized weaponry for *Schützenbrigade* in each Panzer division, 1 January 1940						
	MG 34	s MG 34	5cm le GrW	8cm s GrW	3.7cm PaK	7.5cm le IG
1.PzDiv 1.SchtzBrig in September 1939	84	42	26	18	9	6
1.PzDiv 1.SchtzBrig	101	50	26	24	9	6
2.PzDiv 2.SchtzBrig	101	50	26	24	9	6
3.PzDiv 3.SchtzBrig	101	50	26	24	9	6
4.PzDiv 4.SchtzBrig	180	50	36	24	18	16
5.PzDiv 5.SchtzBrig	232	48	36	24	12	16
6.PzDiv 6.SchtzBrig	220	48	36	24	12	8
7.PzDiv 7.SchtzBrig	257	56	42	30	15	16
8.PzDiv 8.SchtzBrig	220	48	36	24	12	0
9.PzDiv SchtzRgt 10 (SchtzRgt 11)	220	48	36	24	12	16
10.PzDiv 10.SchtzBrig	149	58	33	24	24	16

Production and Allocation of MTW

In 1939, total production of the *Sonderkraftfahrzeug* (SdKfz – special purpose vehicle) 251/1, *mittlere gepanzerter Mannschaftstransportwagen* (m gep MTW – medium armoured personnel carrier) was 537, of which 305 were *ungepanzerte* (ungep – unarmoured) fabricated from mild steel. It was decided at the beginning of 1940 that production was to be concentrated on manufacturing the *gepanzerte* (gep – armoured) type: 116 had been completed by April 1940.

It is possible that some 500 armoured and unarmoured SdKfz 251 had been delivered in time for *Fall Gelb* (Case Yellow), the attack on France in June 1940. The available vehicles were distributed among the sub-units of the rifle regiments according to the valid *Kriegstärkenachtweisungen* (KStN – tables of organization). The actual distribution is unknown, but due to the lack of production it was impossible to equip all tank divisions equally, so it can be assumed that this was left to the discretion of each individual commander.

Only those Panzer divisions commanded by General Guderian (1.PzDiv, 2.PzDiv, 6.PzDiv and 8.PzDiv), since they formed the spearhead of XIX. Armeekorps (mot), received more than two armoured companies.

Before the beginning of *Fall Gelb*, the *Schützenbrigade* (SchtzBrig – rifle brigade) attached to 1.PzDiv received a full establishment of armoured Sdkfz 251 to equip their Schützenregiment (SchtzRgt – rifle regiment) 1. The second rifle regiment in the brigade, SchtzRgt 113, remained equipped with the unarmoured SdKfz 251. [This is confirmed in a rare official document, dated 27 June 1940, in which the authorized allotment of armoured SdKfz 251 was quoted 'at the beginning of the campaign' as 272.] Interestingly, when the campaign ended on 22 June 1940 a total of 241 remained serviceable, and of the 31 vehicles that were not, 17 were written off as a total loss.

Unfortunately, this number is not specified further. The valid KStN, indicates that some of these vehicles would have been the SdKfz 250 light armoured

1. Panzer-Division	/Abt. V	**33**		O.U., den 27. Juni 1940.					
Truppenteil, Dienststelle					Datum				
Meldung über die Kfz.-Lage nach dem Stande vom 26. Juni									1940

1	2	3	4	5	6	7	8	9	10
	Kräder	Kfz. m. Pkw. Fahrgest.	Kfz. m. Lkw. Fahrgest.	3gkw	MTW. m. 3gkw Fahrgest.	Pz. Späh Wagen	Pz. Kampf Wagen	Schul-Pz.	m. s. J.G.
a) Ist-Stärke (bei Einsatzbeginn!)	1433	867	1905	130	272	62	297	16	6
b) von a) einsatzbereit	1011	697	1624	105	241	22	140	4	4
c) von a) nicht einsatzbereit	422	170	281	25	31	40	157	12	2

The vehicle situation of 1.PzDiv as of 25 June 1940.

personnel carrier, but the type did not enter service until May 1941. An MG Kp (gep) was officially authorized to have 18 half-track vehicles: eight were to be SdKfz 250, the rest SdKfz 251. But an order was issued for the SdKfz 250 to be replaced with a similar number of SdKfz 10. Also, an unknown number of armoured SdKfz 251 were substituted by unarmoured versions.

The total of 272 must be considered with great caution. Probably only some 60 percent of these were armoured SdKfz 251, so an unknown number were the unarmoured version. It must not be forgotten that artillery regiment in 1.PzDiv used possibly 24 unarmoured SdKfz 251 as towing tractors for 10.5cm le FH 18. Furthermore, the *Panzerpionier-Kompanie* (armoured engineer company), an integral part of the *Pionier-Bataillon* (engineer battalion), was authorized to have six SdKfz 251 armoured carriers, and these will have been included in the total number.

It was now possible to equip not only the rifle companies, but also the other divisional subunits with the unarmoured or armoured SdKfz 251.

Machine-gun Company

The *Maschinengewehr-Kompanie* (MG-Kp – machine-gun company) 'b' (gp) was a powerful component of the rifle battalion. By May 1940, the company

The sides of the crew compartment on the SdKfz 251 were intentionally made low to reduce the profile of the vehicle on the battlefield. Consequently, the crew would have to keep their heads below the edge in combat.

MG-Kompanie b (gp) (KStN 1116)

SchtzRgt 1, 1. PzDiv as of May 1940

Kp Trupp	1. (MG) Zug	2. (MG) Zug	3. (GrW) Zug	Gefechts-Tross	Inst Trupp	Gepäck-Tross
SdKfz 10	SdKfz 10	SdKfz 10	SdKfz 10	le gl Lkw		
	SdKfz 10	SdKfz 10			Kfz 15	Lkw 3 to
			SdKfz 251	Lkw 3 to		
	SdKfz 251	SdKfz 251	SdKfz 251	Lkw 3 to		
	SdKfz 251	SdKfz 251	SdKfz 251	Lkw 3 to		
Nachr Staffel						
SdKfz 10			SdKfz 251	Lkw 3 to		
SdKfz 10			SdKfz 251	Lkw 3 to		
			SdKfz 251			

was equipped with eight 7.92mm heavy MG 34 with *schwere Lafette* (carriage), tripod-type mounting, for sustained fire and six 8cm *schwerer Granatwerfer* (s GrW – heavy grenade thrower [mortar]) 34. Also, the company was issued with four SdKfz 251 (each mounting two MG 34) and six SdKfz 251 for the *Granatwerfer-Zug* (GrwZg – mortar platoon); the crew was able to fire the dismountable mortar from inside the vehicle, giving them some protection from infantry fire and also shell splinters.

Heavy Company

The *schwere Kompanie* (gep) within the rifle battalion consisted of basic services (HQ section, supply and baggage column) and also a *Hilfstrupp* (support platoon). Three *Teileinheiten* (TE – subunits) provided firepower or engineer support:

TE *Panzer-Abwehr-Zug* (PzAbwZg – tank destroyer platoon) (gep), with three 3.7cm PaK according KStN 1122 (gp),
TE *Infanteriegeschütz-Zug* (gep) (infantry gun platoon), with two 7.5cm le

An SdKfz 251 from 1.PzDiv which has received a direct hit from an enemy anti-tank weapon that ignited the fuel tank below the crew compartment. The fierce heat softened the torsion-bar suspension, causing the vehicle to sag into the ground.

A rifle squad positioned in woodland ready to ambush an enemy patrol. Their main weapon, a 7.92mm *schweres Maschinengewehr* (MG – heavy machine gun) 34 is mounted on a *schweres Lafette* (heavy carriage) 34. As the war progressed, military planners ordered a successive increase in the number of machine guns issued to the rifle regiments. (Ullstein via Getty)

An SdKfz 10/4 towing a
Sonderanhänger (SdAnh
– special purpose trailer)
51 passes along the
main street of a French
town. The SdAnh 51 was
fitted with a removable
container for ammunition.
In certain situations,
the 2cm FlaK 30 could
be dismounted from the
carrier by using the metal
ramps carried across the
front of the vehicle.

IG 18 according to KStN 1123 (gep),
TE *Pionier-Zug* (gep) (engineer platoon) according to KStN 1124 (gep).

The rifle regiments were assigned a variety of tasks, including eliminating border fortifications: vital for the breakthrough in the Ardennes. They were also given the important task of defending the flanks of the spearhead. Wherever tanks could not be deployed, especially in a forest or the tight confines of a village, the riflemen fought from tree to tree or house to house to allow the advance to continue.

The riflemen also played an important role when a river, such as the Meuse [Maas] had to be crossed and then establish a bridgehead before moving on in support of the main attacking force.

Many of the successes achieved by the Panzer divisions would not have been possible without the bravery of the rifle units which, as a consequence, suffered a high ratio of casualties.

The SdKfz 10/5, carrying the 2cm FlaK 38, had a reasonably low profile which made it simpler to conceal on the battlefront, but the small gun shield gave little protection for the crew against fire from enemy infantry.

The 2cm FlaK 38 was designed to have a firing rate of 480 rounds per minute (rpm) and could fire high-explosive ammunition against fortified positions, or armour-piercing to defeat light armoured targets.

Reinforcing the Rifle Brigades

Almost as soon as the *Wehrmacht* was formed, demands began to be made for the rifle brigade to be equipped with more firepower. Initially, apart from grenade launchers [mortars], the riflemen had only a limited number of 7.5cm *leichte Infanteriegeschutz* (le IG – light infantry gun) 18 to provide artillery support.

In 1935, the 15cm *schwere Infanteriegeschütz* (s IG – heavy infantry gun) 33, entered service and initially it was assigned only to the infantry divisions. Those first divisions of the new *Wehrmacht* received a horse-drawn infantry gun company, equipped with six 7.5cm le IG and two 15cm s IG 33 in each regiment. This organization remained in principle unchanged throughout the war, although later the company was motorized.

In 1940, the rifle units in Panzer divisions did not have any artillery weapons, but military planners soon realized this was a serious error. However, their first consideration was to supply the artillery regiment in a Panzer division with a self-propelled howitzer and the rifle regiment with a self-propelled heavy infantry gun. But due to shortage of artillery weapons, their proposal was impossible to implement in the foreseeable future.

After the Polish campaign, the planners initiated a temporary solution: Altmärkische Kettenwerke (Alkett) was contracted to mounted a 15cm s IG 33 on the chassis of an obsolete Pzkpfw I Ausf B. A total of 38 vehicles were built and issued to six self-propelled infantry gun companies, which were attached to six Panzer divisions immediately prior to *Fall Gelb* on 10 May 1940.

> 1.PzDiv with 1.SchtzBrig received s IG Kp (Sfl) 702
> 2.PzDiv with 2.SchtzBrig received s IG Kp (Sfl) 703
> 5.PzDiv with 5.SchtzBrig received s IG Kp (Sfl) 704
> 7.PzDiv with 7.SchtzBrig received s IG Kp (Sfl) 705
> 9.PzDiv with 9.SchtzBrig received s IG Kp (Sfl) 701
> 10.PzDiv with 10.SchtzBrig received s IG Kp (Sfl) 706

Although the rifle units welcomed this extra firepower, the PzKpfw I Ausf B chassis proved to be underpowered, overloaded and mechanically unreliable (see *Panzerartillerie*: Osprey 2019).

After-action Reports

After the capitulation of France, all Panzer divisions were ordered to submit detailed after-action reports and also to complete a standardized questionnaire regarding organizational issues, tactics and weaponry. Sadly, the combat experiences of the rifle brigades, regiments, battalions and companies is somewhat under-represented in these records.

During the *Blitzkrieg* on France, the rifle units would enter combat for the first time equipped with larger numbers of armoured personnel carriers.

A newly delivered SdKfz 251/5 issued to the *Pionier-Zug* (Pi-Zg – pioneer platoon) in a rifle unit. The letter 'Y', under the tactical marking, indicates that the vehicle is in service with 7.PzDiv.

It is thought that the majority of unarmoured SdKfz 251 halftracks were used as artillery tractors for towing (as here) the 10.5cm *leichter Feldhaubitze* (le FH – light field howitzer) 18 in the divisional artillery regiment.

The newly formed 'Motorisierte Gruppe von Kleist' (Motorized Group von Kleist) – later 1.Panzerarmee – combined half of the Panzer divisions, including XIX.Armeekorps commanded by Guderian and XXXXI.Armeekorps commanded by Georg-Hans Rheinhardt. In the first phase, both were tasked with crossing the border in the Ardennes, to form an armoured spearhead to advance rapidly to the north coast of France and Belgium.

The group produced a report which shows that at the beginning of *Fall Gelb*, the five Panzer divisions, two infantry divisions (mot) and an independent infantry regiment (Grossdeutschland) had the following combined vehicle strength:

12,158 Motorcycles	9,009 Passenger Cars
16,745 Trucks	167 Buses
1,047 Half-track Tractors	107 Personnel Carriers (unarmoured)
105 Trailers	35 Flatbed Trailers (tank transport)
216 PzKpfw I	461 PzKpfw II
461 PzKpfw II	322 PzKpfw III
141 PzKpfw IV	111 PzBefWg (command tanks)
154 Personnel Carriers (armoured)	362 Armoured Cars

The great discrepancies in quantities between this report and the report from 1.PzDiv cannot be explained.

The report culminated in demands for improvements:

Effective armour protection for our tanks and also for the 'absolutely inadequate' armoured cars.

Increased performance from our anti-tank guns.

Introduction of self-propelled artillery and tank destroyer units.

Increased supply of bridging equipment.

Improvement and simplification of bridge-layer vehicles.

Modification and improvement of *Ladungsleger* (demolition charge carrier).

Increase the number of *Flammenwerfer* (flamethrowers) within the *Pionier-Kompanie* (PiKp – engineer company).

For some unknown reason the SdKfz 251 personnel carrier is not mentioned.

During a march, the crew of an SdKfz 10/4 sat on the gun platform – only the driver and commander had cushioned seats. The vehicle carried 12 magazines, each containing 12 rounds of 2cm ammunition: a total of 240.

The box-shaped container fitted to the *Sonderanhänger* (SdAnh – special purpose trailer) 51 was used to carry 32 magazines, each holding 20 rounds of 2cm ammunition.

The report also noted how the rifle elements should liaise with tank units in a Panzer division:

> When cooperating with tanks, it has once again been shown that the tank assault requires an in-depth consultation between the commanders of tank and rifle units. Each needs to be fully briefed on their target before the attack. Many assaults by the SchtzRgt conducted without support from tanks or assault guns, often ended in failure and a significant loss of personnel.

One of the few available documents submitted from regimental level was delivered by SchtzRgt 4 (6.PzDiv):

> 30 May 1940
> In the course of the morning, III./SchtzRgt 4 has pushed some 3km north from the accommodation area west of Abeele [Abele]. The terrain, densely covered with hedges and woodland, is even more difficult to observe because of the misty conditions. As a

result, scattered enemy groups are still concealed behind the frontline in thickets and woodland. Unexpectedly, individual vehicles in the battalion are hit and we suffer losses. The gep MTW with 11.Kp proves to be immune against infantry fire.

3 June 1940

During the evening, III./SchRgt 4 marched to the Vaudringhem assembly area. This was very demanding on the drivers due to it being carried out in complete darkness. In addition, the enemy had blasted many of the bridges, which made detours necessary. The route went through the middle of the coal-mining area in northern France and took us over historic ground; the battlefields of previous wars. The personnel carriers of II./SchRgt 4 suffered a lot of mechanical damage; the lack of rubber pads caused the vehicles to be run on bare tracks for long periods, resulting in numerous failures.

4 June 1940.

At 09:10hrs the division issued orders to prepare for marching at 12:00hrs. Mission: pursuit of the enemy to the south, bypassing the fortified villages. At 18:00hrs, after a six-hour postponement, the battalion began the second night march. Apart from 11./SchtzRgt 4, where damage to the halftracks became more and more frequent, the battalion reached the ruins of Nouzonville, west of the river Meuse [Maas], with almost no breakdowns. Here the vehicles are to undergo a thorough inspection and maintenance.

The available space in a SdKfz 10/4 for personal weapons and effects was extremely limited. Consequently, three *Karabiner* (K – carbine [rifle]) 98k were carried in racks on each of the front mudguards. The metal ramps used to dismount the gun are fitted across the front of the halftrack.

Two SdKfz 251/5 carry the 'oak leaf' symbol of 1.PzDiv and also the tactical marking for a *Pionier-Zug* (Pi-Zg – engineer platoon).

An SdKfz 251, towing a 10.5cm le FH 18, crosses a bridge assembled by the Pi-Abt using pontoons and trusses to carry a *Brückengerät* (bridging section) 'B'. The sections could be assembled to cross widths of 51.40m (24,385kg capacity), 83.50m (12,193kg capacity) or 120.30m (4,064kg capacity).

5 June 1940

At 09:10hrs, the division ordered combat readiness for 12:00hrs. The battalion commander considered whether 11.Kp should lead the attack despite having reached the limits of combat readiness; half of their halftracks had mechanically failed, and the remainder were barely serviceable. The battalion commander requested replacement vehicles, including Kfz 70, from the other battalion. Fortunately the attack was postponed at 15:00hrs.

7 June 1940

With great difficulty 11./SchtzRgt 4 converted to wheeled vehicles (Kfz 70). All units in the regiment donated a variety of vehicle types to 11.Kp. Those halftracks which could not be made combat ready with the available means, were left under guard in Nouzonville.

The initial equipment of SchtzRgt 4 (within SchtzBrig 6 attached to 6.PzDiv) was some 15 armoured SdKfz 251, sufficient to equip 11.Kp.

Entries in the war diary of the regiment confirm the large number of mechanical problems they experienced when the armoured SdKfz 251 entered service. The type was built on the chassis of an SdKfz 11 half-track tractor. This versatile tractor used lubricated metal tracks fitted with massive rubber pads which allowed the vehicle to be driven at high speed over firm terrain without damaging the tracks and suspension. But the tracks required constant maintenance; the rubber pads were extremely susceptible to abrasion and when worn down they had to be changed immediately or the track links could break.

The most reported mechanical fault with the SdKfz 251 was track damage. The problem was exacerbated by the supply of replacement pads being insufficient to meet the demand from maintenance units. The same problem affected artillery and other units operating the type.

After the French campaign, 10.PzDiv completed a questionnaire issued by the general staff:

Special questions for Panzer divisions:

Have our basic principles regarding leadership, deployment and combat by tank units proved their worth?

Answer: If the divisional commander is detached from the commanding squadron, he must have two armoured radio-equipped vehicles.

Whether a Panzer or a rifle brigade was deployed as the spearhead of an attack depended on the tactical situation and terrain. In the majority of cases, support of the riflemen by attached tank companies was necessary. But this cooperation requires further training.

Destroyed French and German military vehicles litter the road near a small town in the Ardennes. An SdKfz 251 from 1.PzDiv has received a hit from an anti-tank gun which has blown the front-axle assembly off the chassis, but the *Panzeraufbau* (armoured body) appears to be intact.

An SdKfz 10/4 of 7.PzDiv has been deployed to fire at a distant pocket of enemy resistance. The 2cm FlaK 30 was an accurate weapon which had an effective range of over 4,000m. (Ullstein via Getty)

Far left: A *Kradschützen-Kompanie* (motorcycle company) lined up on a narrow lane in France. The unit had an extraordinary tactical mobility, particularly on the well-made roads in northern Europe, and were well armed with light and heavy machine guns and also the 8cm *leichter Granatwerfer* (le GrW – grenade launcher[mortar]) 34.

Left: The *Funkkraftwagen* (FuKw – radio vehicle) Kfz 2, was built on an *Einheitsfahrgestell für leichte Personenkraftwagen* (universal chassis for light passenger cars). Although the type was highly manoeuvrable – due to all-wheel drive and steering – it was mechanically complicated and consequently expensive to manufacture.

However, the prerequisite for the successful deployment of the Panzer brigade lay in the concentration of the armoured forces (except those tanks directly attached to the rifle units). To effectively follow the advancing tanks attack, the supporting artillery must be issued with self-propelled guns. There should be sufficient forward observers and also command tanks for the artillery liaison.

To accompany the tank attack, the brigade was successfully assigned self-propelled 4.7cm *Panzerjäger*, a *Schützenkompanie* and a *Panzer-Pionierkompanie*, both equipped with armoured halftracks.

The answer to a further question is interesting, though, again, the armoured personnel carrier is not mentioned specifically:

Which weapons proved to be especially effective?
Answer: The rifle brigade placed great emphasis on the MG 34, the s 8cm GrW 36 and also the 15cm sIG 33.

The armoured half-track carrier received a positive mention in the section dealing with field medical services:

The front-line units should be issued with two *Krankenkraftwagen* [KrKw – ambulance] – previously one KrKw – for each *Panzer-Abteilung*, *Schützen-Bataillon*, *Pionier-Bataillon* and *Aufklärungs-Abteilung*. During the campaign a shortage of KrKw was made up from our stock of captured vehicles.

The armoured personnel carrier has proven to be very useful for the Panzer regiment when searching for and transporting the wounded from the battlefield. Four armoured KrKw are required for each regiment.

In this long report regarding performance and suitability, almost every German infantry weapon, artillery piece and tank are mentioned; but not the SdKfz 251. The reason could be that very few armoured SdKfz 251 personnel carriers had been produced, but it is possible that the usually efficient German documentation was not kept up to date – or simply that high command echelons, perhaps even division officers were not aware that an armoured personnel carrier was available to front-line units. Military planners may have mistakenly identified the half-track personnel carrier as an infantry transport.

Written in the margin of the original document is an interesting detail: it shows the position of 1.PzDiv in the Victory Parade by German forces in Paris on 14 June 1940 – the city was treated as a non-belligerent zone until the armistice was signed at Compiegne on 22 June 1940. The commander of

the division, *Generalleutnant* Friedrich Kirchner, insisted on the participation of a SchtzKp with 21 SdKfz 251. Interestingly, this was more than the number authorized detailed in the relevant KStN.

The crew compartment of an SdKfz 251. Note the complicated, and space consuming, hinges for the rear doors.

Changing Tactics

In contrast to conventional infantry, *Schützen* supplied with armoured personnel carriers were able to fulfil a wider variety of combat missions.

Those units not issued with the type would be transported – as close as safety allowed – to the battlefront, where they would dismount and deploy. But as foot soldiers they would not able to keep pace with the rapidly advancing armoured forces. After completing a combat mission, the infantrymen were forced to wait for their vehicles so as to follow the tank assault. When the tanks breached the enemy lines, the lack of rifle infantry often brought the advance to a halt as tank crews fought enemy counterattacks.

Well-planned cooperation between the *Schützen* and tank units was a prerequisite for success on the battlefront, since only the armoured halftracks enabled the rifle regiment to follow the tank force to keep the momentum of the spearhead rolling.

5

1941 – NEW CHALLENGES

In 1940, the *gepanzerter Mannschaftstransportwagen* (armoured personnel carrier) officially became known as the *Schützenpanzerwagen* (SPW – armoured personnel carrier), but both continued to be used in official documents and also by troops in the field. The acronym SPW was commonly used by unit commanders.

Organizational Changes

After the end of the French campaign, German military planners initiated a programme to increase the number of Panzer divisions from ten to 20. Their 'miracle' solution was to reduce the number of tanks allotted to a division by some 50 percent. Each of five divisions – 1.PzDiv, 2.PzDiv, 4.PzDiv, 5.PzDiv and 10.PzDiv – had to relinquish a tank regiment, which were then assigned to form new units. A further four tank regiments were newly formed using men and vehicles from *Panzer-Ersatzabteilungen* (PzErsAbt – training and replacement battalions).

Although the combat strength of each division appears to have been weakened, military planners considered that they had significantly increased the fighting ability of a Panzer division, since the majority were now equipped with PzKpfw III, PzKpfw 35(t), PzKpfw 38(t) and PzKpfw IV.

However, the reduction in numbers negated some aspects of the original plan for the massed deployment of tanks to break through at focal points during an attack. This approach now had to be carefully planned and field commanders made aware of expected losses.

The *Schützenbrigaden* (rifle brigades) in newly established Panzer divisions corresponded approximately to existing units. In early 1940, it was decided to form a fourth rifle company for each of the four battalions in a regiment to improve combat effectiveness.

Commander of the *Deutsches Afrika Korps* (DAK), Generalleutnant Erwin Rommel was a conspicuous user of an armoured personnel carrier and was often seen close to a battlefront in an SdKfz 250/3 *Funkwagen* (FuWg – radio vehicle).

In 1941, the combat value of an individual rifle unit was significantly improved, since each regiment received an infantry gun company equipped with four 7.5cm *leichte Infanteriegeschütz* (le IG – light infantry gun) 18 and two 15cm *schwere Infanteriegeschütz* (s IG – heavy infantry gun) 33.

The *Schützen* brigades in 1.PzDiv, 2.PzDiv, 5.PzDiv, 7.PzDiv, 9.PzDiv and 10.PzDiv were allowed to retain their *Selbstfahrlafette* (Sfl – self-propelled)

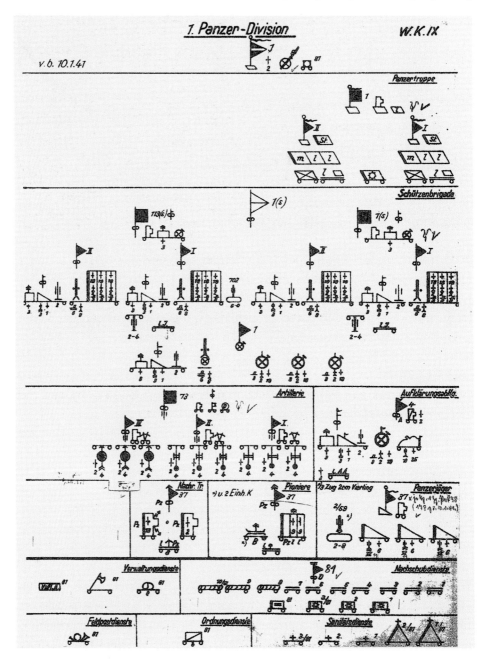

The *Sonderanhänger* (SdAnh – special purpose trailer) 115 had a load-carrying capacity of 15,000kg, sufficient for the recovery of light armoured vehicles: here an SdKfz 251/6.

heavy infantry gun companies, each equipped with six 15cm *schweres Infanteriegeschutz* 33 auf PzKpfw I Ausf B.

Most *Schützen* brigades in the 20 Panzer divisions had a *Kradschützen-Bataillon* (motorcycle rifle battalion) which were organized according to the current KStN, but with occasional deviations.

First Waffen-SS Units

Hitler had always planned to create the Waffen-SS, a political army, and the following units were declared combat ready in early 1941:

SS-Division Das Reich
SS-Division Totenkopf
SS-Division (mot) Germania – later Wiking

All were organized with conventional infantry regiments and had no *motorisierte* (mot – motorized) battalions.

Production of Armoured Personnel Carriers

Although the German *Rüststand* (armaments) tables, which were published monthly, listed all German weapons and vehicles currently in production, finding the exact number of SdKfz 250 and SdKfz 251 built is not possible.

In combat, the crew of an SdKfz 10/4 had drop-down side panels on the gun mounting bed so that it could be traversed. The 2cm FlaK was magazine-fed by hand, requiring an agile and well-trained trained loader.

For reasons unknown, the method of collating the numbers was changed several times as production continued.

In September 1940, the figures for the number of personnel carriers being manufactured were included with those for the SdKfz 10 and SdKfz 11 half-tracked tractors; the chassis of both types were used for the personnel carriers. This method of counting continued until the end of 1941. The only 'reliable' production data for the light and medium personnel carriers is in documents emanating from the *Inspekteur der Panzertruppe* 6 (Insp d PzTrp – weapons department for armoured forces).

An interesting document originating from Insp 6 and dated 10 June 1941, contains a demand from the Panzer divisions, which were in the process of reorganization, for armoured cars and 316 SdKfz 250 and 238 SdKfz 251 personnel carriers. But the document clearly states that only 150 of each type would be available.

Examination of the *Waffenamt* entries, from June 1939 up until the end of production in 1941, reveals that a total of 305 unarmoured SdKfz 251 and 645 armoured SdKfz 251 had been delivered.

After numerous delays, production of the SdKfz 250 finally began in May 1941 and, according to *Waffenamt* documentation, a total of 389 vehicles had been delivered by the end of the year.

In February 1942, the SdKfz 251 and the SdKfz 250 were listed individually in the *Rüststand* tables, now including the number of vehicles actually available and those held in stock, dating back to November 1941.

But there is a significant discrepancy. In November 1941, the total number of available SdKfz 250 (888) exceeds the numbers (247) produced. It is logical to assume they include those for the *leichte gepanzerte Munitionskraftwagen* (le gep MunKw – light armoured ammuniton carrier [SdKfz 252]) and the

The Kfz 4 *Truppenluft-schutzwagen* (anti-aircraft defence vehicle,) was based on the light passenger car produced by Stöwer. The *Zwillingssockel-Lafette* (ZwiSoLa – twin mounting) MG 34 was installed in the rear. The vehicle is in service with Leibstandarte-SS Adolf Hitler, which was an infantry brigade in 1941.

	SdKfz 251 production	SdKfz 250 production	SdKfz 251 stock	SdKfz 250 stock
Until November 1941	885	269	-	-
November 1941	48	78	750	888
December 1941	70	64	803	991
January 1942	55	77	883	1,052
February 1942	86	100	860	1,104
March 1942	95	112	1,034	1,212
April 1942	82	183	1,087	1,312
May 1942	82	95	1,321*	721
June 1942	95	84	1,608*	870
July 1942	105	31	1,761*	952
August 1942	132	157	1,801*	1,133
September 1942	120	169	3,131**	
October 1942	94	119	3,357**	
November 1942	125	126	3,569**	
December 1942	129	121	3,829**	

* Calculated: ** Actual stock from September 1942.

Elements of 6.PzDiv: An SdKfz 251/10 mounting a 3.7cm *Panzerabwehrkanone* (PaK – anti-tank gun), fitted with a standard gun shield, and a PzKpfw IV Ausf E pass through a burning Russian village.

leichte gepanzerte Beobachtungskraftwagen (le gep BeobKw – light armoured observation vehicle [SdKfz 253]) since both used the same chassis. Both vehicles were purpose-built for the *Sturmartillerie* (StuArt – assault artillery) and had been in production since the beginning of 1940 – long before SdKfz 250. If the production figures for both types (413 and 285 respectively) are added together, then the November 1941 stock seems plausible; any differences can be explained by losses at the front.

In May 1942, the method of counting was changed again; *Rüststand* table G219 now listed the SdKfz 250 and SdKfz 251 and all other armoured MTW (all other armoured MTW possibly indicates the few armoured SdKfz 8 prime movers that were built).

At first, table G219/1 listed the SdKfz 250; table G219/2 listed the SdKfz 251, but for an unknown reason the method of counting was again changed in September 1942. Now table G219 listed only the total production and stocks of both types.

July 1941: A motorcycle combination-mounted 8cm *leichter Granatwerfer* (le GrWrf – light grenade launcher [mortar]) 34 team hunkered down in a roadside ditch near the town of Livani, Latvia. (Ullstein via Getty)

Above: Christmas 1942 in the desert: Two SdKfz 251 from the staff section of 15.PzDiv; the unit had been forced to retreat to Tunisia after the second battle of El Alamein. The halftrack to the right is an SdKfz 251/6 *Kommandowagen* (KdoWg – command vehicle).

Right: During the first months of the desert war, Rommel used an ex-Italian army four-wheeled caravan as his personal accommodation. The heavy trailer was towed by an SdKfz 251/6.

An SdKfz 10/4, in service with FlaKBtl (mot) 602 which was attached to 4.Panzerarmee when *Unternehmen* Barbarossa was launched on 22 June 1941.

Any clear assignment to a single unit is not possible; the available records do not allow us to determine the exact number of available armoured and unarmoured SdKfz 251 in the individual Panzer divisions.

The few available strength reports for this period show different counting methods, in most cases the numbers for *Rad-Panzerspähwagen* (wheeled armoured car), *Schützenpanzerwagen* and artillery observation vehicles were added together.

The Balkan Campaign

In April 1941, despite the ongoing process of reorganizing the tank divisions, Adolf Hitler ordered his forces to launch *Unternehmen* (Operation) Marita, the invasion of Yugoslavia and Greece. Five – 2.PzDiv, 5.PzDiv, 9.PzDiv, 11.PzDiv and 14.PzDiv – of the six tank divisions deployed had already disbanded their tank brigades and now had only two tank regiments each equipped with the 5cm-armed PzKpfw III. The exception was 8.PzDiv which retained the authorized three regiments, since it was equipped with the 3.7cm-armed PzKpfw 38(t).

The exact number of rifle regiments equipped with personnel carriers is not known, but it is most unlikely that more than one rifle company (gp) was assigned to each regiment. The war diaries of 2.PzDiv and 14.PzDiv make no mention of being supplied with armoured personnel carriers.

Above: An SdKfz 250/1, fitted with a *schwere Machinengewehr* (s MG – heavy machine gun) 34 was one of a number, sent in early 1943, to reinforce *Panzerarmee Afrika*. The vehicle is in service with PzRgt 8 of 10.PzDiv.

Right: A regular supply of water and fuel was vital for mobile desert warfare. This SdKfz 251/6 *Kommandowagen* (KdoWg – command vehicle) carries jerrycans of both in a rack on the side of the superstructure. Those filled with water were marked with a prominent white cross.

Above: The designation SdKfz 10/4 was changed to SdKfz 10/5, when the 2cm FlaK 30 was replaced by the 2cm FlaK 38. The rate of fire could be varied from 280 to 480rpm and gunners were encouraged to fire short bursts.

Left: The crew of this SdKfz 10/4 has dug a depression into the desert sand to conceal its vehicle. The windscreen has been covered to prevent it reflecting the sun and the gun has been draped with a blanket to protect it from the omnipresent dust.

Above: The SturmFlak was a small vehicle, meaning that only personal equipment and a limited amount of ammunition could be transported on board. Consequently, the SdAnh 51 was essential to carry additional magazines.

Right: An SdKfz 251/1 carries a Nazi flag – red with a black Swastika on a white disk – to identify it as friendly to patrolling *Luftwaffe* aircraft.

Left: The 20-round magazines containing ammunition for the 2cm FlaK guns were often criticized by crews, since they could be easily damaged, causing the gun to jam.

Below: A surprisingly large number of SdKfz 251 were fitted with an improvised frame-type antenna to convert a troop carrier to serve as a *Kommandowagen* (KdoWg – command vehicle).

Above: The front-axle assembly on all German halftracks was mechanically vulnerable to damage and time consuming to repair or replace.

Right: German workshop units were issued with light passenger cars, such as the Stöwer-built Kfz 2/40 cross-country vehicle. A lack of cranes meant that engineers had to improvise – here they have simply rolled a heavy passenger car on its side to effect a repair.

North Africa

Adolf Hitler had decided to intervene in North Africa in support of his ally Mussolini, and issued orders for two Panzer divisions to be sent to Tunisia in February 1941.

The 5.leichte Division (motorisiert) (le Div [mot] – light division-motorized) – later redesignated 21.PzDiv – had a strong tank regiment (PzRgt 5) with 71 PzKpfw III and 20 PzKpfw IV. The unit was assigned Infanterieregiment (InfRgt – infantry regiment) 200, with two *Maschinengewehr-Abteilungen* (MG-Abt – machine-gun battalions). According to the relevant KStN, each battalion was supplied with ten SdKfz 251.

The 15.PzDiv was organized as a standard German tank division and had a rifle regiment with two rifle battalions and a motorcycle rifle battalion. The exact number of personnel carriers delivered is not documented, but an indication is given in a *Waffenamt* memorandum, dated 10 June 1941:

All of the following vehicles must be mechanically prepared for use in hot-climate (desert) conditions:

220 le SPW [SdKfz 250]
160 m SPW [SdKfz 251]

An SdKfz 251 with a number of 'modifications': The visor over the right-hand side vision aperture has been replaced with a welded-on steel plate and a very simple 'frame antenna' has been constructed by the crew from wooden sticks and wire. A *Scherenfernrohr* (Sf – scissors periscope) is visible next to the MG shield.

Above: The tactical marking painted on the front plate of this SdKfz 250, indicates that it is in service with a *Pionier-Zug* (engineer platoon). It is being followed by an SdKfz 251/5 Ausf C.

Right: A well-camouflaged SdKfz 251/1 fitted with a *schwere Wurfgerät* (large launching device) 40: a *Wurfrahmen* (launching frame) carried up to six 28cm or 32cm *Wurfkörper* (rocket missile) in their *Packkiste* (carrying crate). The yellow-painted crossed letter 'Y' symbol indicates that it is from 16.PzDiv.

The vehicles were almost certainly intended for use in North Africa, but it is doubtful if such a large number of half-track personnel carriers was ever delivered to the *Deutsches Afrika Korps* (DAK).

During more than two years of battle, DAK units generated a vast number of reports which, very precisely, describe the suitability and reliability of German weapons and vehicles in desert conditions. Even captured equipment is often referred to in after-action reports, including the British Ordnance Quick Firing (OQF) 25-pounder field guns – in German service the 8.76cm *Kanonen-Haubitze* (*englisch*), (KanHaub [e] – canon-howitzer [English]) – which was highly valued by Rommel and his artillery commanders.

But no reports regarding the use and serviceability of the *Schützenpanzer* in North Africa can be found.

The Soviet Union

In the first phase of *Unternehmen* Barbarossa, German tank divisions rapidly advanced over enormous distances and captured vast areas of Soviet territory. Tank crews and infantry of the retreating Red Army fought bravely, but on many occasions were encircled and annihilated.

An SdKfz 251/1 from Heeresgruppe Nord (Army Group North) crosses a railway line in Latvia as German forces advance towards Leningrad in 1941. Note the vehicle is fitted with a large map table.

The medical section of SS-PzDiv Totenkopf relied, like many other units, on a heavy motorcycle combination to provide instant treatment, or the rapid transport of wounded troops from the battlefield. (Ullstein via Getty)

Above: A *Zug-Führer* (platoon leader) has positioned his SdKfz 251/10, armed with a 3.7cm PaK, on the bank of a river to protect a pioneer battalion which is constructing a bridge.

Left: A dispatch rider observes the tanks of a Panzer division advance, being followed by an SdKfz 267, *grosser Panzerbefehlswagen* (gr PzBeflWg – large armoured command vehicle) and an SdKfz 253 artillery observation vehicle. Note a 5cm PaK 38 has been positioned for long-range anti-tank fire.

Above: A crew member of an armoured carrier from 16.PzDiv fuses a *Wurfkörper* rocket for firing.

Right: Before firing, the impact fuses had to be inserted. The simple *Packkiste* (carrying crates) were mostly fabricated from wood, but some were metal. The 28cm *Wurfkörper* (*Spreng*) was high-explosive and the 32cm *Wurfkörper* (*Flamm*) an incendiary missile.

German infantry divisions and rifle units quickly learned to appreciate the impact of the Panzer units.

The number of infantry fighting vehicles supplied to the rifle units was still insufficient; as a rule each Panzer division had only one *Schützenkompanie* (gp). A good example is 5.PzDiv which, after being restructured several times, was transferred to the *Ost* (East) Front in September 1941. On 27 September, the division submitted a strength report stating that it had the authorized complement of 27 armoured personnel carriers:

Two SdKfz 250
14 SdKfz 251/1
Six SdKfz 251/5
Three SdKfz 251/6
Two SdKfz 251/8

This covered the strength of a *Schützenkompanie* according to KStN 1114 (gp) and a PzPiZg (gp) according to KStN 1124 (gp). The division was also supplied with 22 *leichte gepanzerter Beobachtungswagen* (le gep BeobKw – light armoured artillery observer vehicles), mainly SdKfz 250/5 but also some SdKfz 253 and a few SdKfz 254, wheel-cum-track vehicles.

The 28cm *Wurfkörper* (*Spreng*) had an effective range of between 975m and 1,925m; for safety reasons, it was not permitted to fire at a target less than 750m distant. The 30cm *Wurfkörper*, which entered service in 1942, had a considerably increased range of 4,550m.

A German machine-gun team covers a road junction from the 'safety' of their fox hole near a disabled Russian T-26 tank. The MG 34 required special care during the *Rasputitsa* (season of mud), since dirt or frost would often cause the weapon to jam. (Ullstein via Getty Images)

Above: An SdKfz 10/5 following advancing armoured rifle units. Note the long box which carries a replacement gun barrel.

Right: The cargo box on the *Sonderanhänger* (SdAnh – special purpose trailer) 51 carried 20 pre-loaded magazines of 2cm ammunition.

The riflemen of a *Schützenkompanie* (gp), could keep in close contact with the advancing armour and rapidly intervene when infantry support was needed.

Conversely, those transported in Kfz 70 or other standard soft-skinned vehicles, such as a 3-ton truck, would have to keep a safe distance between themselves and the attacking tanks. It was not unusual for riflemen to mount tanks following in the second wave. But here they were vulnerable, and many units suffered severe losses if the enemy counterattacked with fire from anti-tank or machine guns.

By autumn 1941, several months of battle had created a better understanding, between the commanders of tank and the rifle units, of tactical and operational methods. As a result, cooperation significantly improved.

On 12 December 1941, the Battle of Moscow ended after Russian forces, commanded by General Zhukov, counterattacked and captured Solechnaya Gora, some 40km northwest of the city. The remnants of the once-invincible German divisions were forced to dig in and survive the winter.

Two SturmFlaK provide support fire for an assault by armoured infantry. The gun commander observes the results, while the loader provides a steady supply of pre-loaded magazines of 2cm ammunition.

Above: An SdKfz 251/6 *Kommandowagen* (KdoWg – command vehicle) has been fitted with an improvised radio antenna. Note the 8m *Kurbelmast* (telescopic mast) is protected by a canvas cover.

Right: Barely camouflaged with whitewash, this SdKfz 10/4 has the gun dismounting ramps stowed on the front of the vehicle.

An SdKfz 251 Ausf A in service as a command post. The large map table was only fitted for a short period during the invasion of France, but a number did survive long into the war.

6

1941 – VARIANTS

The *Heereswaffenamt* (Army Ordnance Office) had, from the very beginning, planned to develop different versions of the SdKfz 250 and SdKfz 251. Both types would be delivered from the manufacturer fitted with *Grundhalter* (basic holders) before *Zusatzhalter* (additional holders), weaponry and special equipment was fitted in accordance with their tactical purpose as defined in the respective *Kriegstärkenachtweisung* (KStN – organizational structure).

All versions were to be equipped with a *Funkgerät* (FuG – radio device) which was installed in front of the co-driver and allowed voice communication at 2km to 3km range. In 1942 an improved radio began to be fitted, the *Funksprech* (FuSpr – transceiver) 'f' which had a voice range of some 6km to 8km.

In 1939, the medium armoured troop carrier entered production as the *Sonderkraftfahrzeug* (SdKfz – special purpose vehicle) 251 and was first used in Poland, then, more extensively, for the invasion of France. An *Allgemeine Heeres-Mitteilungen* (general army bulletin), issued on 16 November 1940, contains a list of all variants and confirmation of it now being designated as a *Schützenpanzerwagen* (SPW – armoured personnel carrier).

SdKfz 251

The SdKfz 251/1 *mittlerer Schützenpanzerwagen* (m SPW – medium armoured personnel carrier) was the most numerous produced and equipped *Schützenkompanie* 'b' (gp) according KStN 1114 (gp).

The vehicle was designed to carry a *Schützengruppe* (rifle squad) of ten men plus a *Gruppenführer* (squad commander) and a driver. The vehicle was armed with three *Maschinengewehr* (MG – machine gun) 34 and two *Maschinenpistole* (MP – machine pistol [submachine gun]) 38 or MP 40. One MG 34 was

The heavy company in a PzGenBtl (gp) was authorized to have three anti-tank guns. These would be towed by a medium armoured personnel carrier such as an SdKfz 251 Ausf D. The vehicle is from an unknown Waffen-SS unit, and has a 2.8cm *schwere Panzerbüchse* (s PzB – heavy anti-tank rifle) 41 mounted in place of the machine gun.

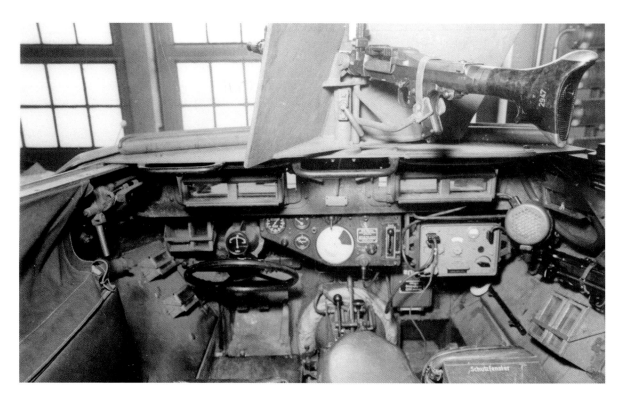

Above: The driver's position of the SdKfz 250 was almost identical to that of the SdKfz 251. The MG 34 has been secured in its travel rest, which would be folded to the side so that the weapon could be used.

Right: The SdKfz 251/1 was the standard armoured personnel carrier. The driver sat on the left-hand side and the radio operator on the right with a *Funksprech* (FuSprech – transceiver) 'f'.

mounted at the front of the open superstructure and protected by a small *Panzerschild* (armour shield), another could be fitted on a pivot-type mounting at the rear of the body and used for anti-aircraft fire; the third machine gun was carried inside the vehicle. The *Karabiner* (carbine [rifle]) 98k for the riflemen were carried in racks.

The SdKfz 251/1 had space for two heavy MG 34 teams and their equipment. A heavy MG 34 could be mounted; the standard MG and armoured shield were removed to allow a *schwere Maschinengewehr Lafette für MG 34*, a heavy shock-absorbing gun mount and *Winkelfernrohr* (periscopic gunsight), to be clamped on the visor plate.

An early production SdKfz 251 Ausf A, recognizable by the number of vision apertures along the side of the superstructure. The *Panzerschild* (armour shield) for the front MG was not a standard item.

SdKfz 251/2

This *Granatwerferwagen* (GrW – grenade launcher [mortar] vehicle) was deployed with the *schwere Kompanie* (s Kp – heavy company) attached to the rifle battalion. It carried an 8cm *schwere Granatwerfer* (s GrW – heavy grenade launcher [mortar]), 66 rounds of ammunition and a crew of eight, including a driver. The weapon was normally fired from inside the vehicle using a fixed base plate. A standard *Bodenplatte* (base plate) was also carried for the weapon to be dismounted. The SdKfz 251/2 was armed with a single MG 34 and an MP 38 or MP 40.

Above: In 1942, when production of the SdKfz 251 Ausf C began, the engine cooling vents were fitted with armoured covers. The vehicle is fitted a 2m rod antenna indicating that is equipped with a FuSprech 'f' transceiver.

Right: In 1943, the SdKfz 251 Ausf D entered production with a redesigned (simplified) *Panzeraufbau* (armoured body).

Above: This SdKfz 251/1 Ausf C was one of those used to transport Adolf Hitler to the *Wolfschanze* (Wolf's Lair), some 8km from Rastenburg in East Prussia (Poland). This was one of several *Führer-Hauptquartier* (leader's headquarters) that were built in Central and Eastern Europe.

Left: General Walther Nehring, here in an SdKfz 251/6 *Kommandowagen* (KdoWg – command vehicle), commanded 18.PzDiv during *Unternehmen* Barbarossa and later *Unternehmen* Taifun (Operation *Typhoon*).

Above: A mortar crew prepares to fire from an SdKfz 251/2, 8cm *Granatwerferwagen* (grenade launcher [mortar] carrier). The type was built using the SdKfz 251 Ausf C and this vehicle is one of a small batch with a riveted – not welded – *Panzeraufbau*.

Right: The 8cm GrW 34 was mounted on a rigid plate in the SdKfz 251/2. A standard *Bodenplatte* (base plate) was used when the weapon was dismounted from the carrier.

SdKfz 251/3

In 1940, this vehicle was issued to heavy infantry companies as a *mittlerer Schutzenpanzerwagen für leichte Infanteriegeschütz* (m SPW fur le IG – medium armoured carrier for light infantry gun) to tow the 7.5cm le IG 18. The vehicle carried a crew of seven and a small amount of ammunition. Somewhat confusingly, the same designation was applied to a *Funkwagen* (radio vehicle) which entered service in 1943.

SdKfz 251/4

This variant was originally designated as an ammunition carrier to support the SdKfz 251/3, but it later became a prime mover for 7.5cm *leichte Infanteriegeschütz* (le IG – light infantry gun) 18 and *Panzerabwehrkanone* (PaK – anti-tank gun) 38 and 40.

SdKfz 251/5

This *mittlerer Schützenpanzerwagen* (*Pionier*) (m SPW [Pi] – medium armoured personnel carrier [engineers]) was issued to the engineer platoon of the heavy

An SdKfz 251/4 Ausf C towing a 7.5cm *leichter Infanteriegeschütz* (le IG – light infantry gun) 18.

Above: The SdKfz 251/7 was a specialized engineer vehicle issued to the *Panzer-Pionier-Bataillon* (PzPiBtl – armoured engineer battalion) of the PzDiv. In contrast to the SdKfz 251/5, it carried a bridging section on each side of the superstructure. The vehicle is towing a 2.8cm s PzB 41 on a *Sonderanhänger* (SdAnh – special purpose trailer) 32/3.

Right: This SdKfz 251/10 has struck a mine, which has destroyed the front-axle assembly and damaged the engine bay.

company in a rifle battalion and carried specialized equipment for engineers, which included tools and explosive charges. Three different sub-versions with alternating pioneer equipment were available. The vehicle carried an eight-man crew and was armed with two MG 34, two machine pistols and a 7.92mm *Panzerbüchse* (PzB – anti-tank rifle) 39.

SdKfz 251/6

This *mittlerer Kommando-Panzerwagen* (m Kdo PzW – medium armoured command vehicle) was used by senior officers, including Guderian and others in higher command echelons. The type was fitted with the large and conspicuous *Rahmenantenne* (frame antenna), which made it easy for the enemy to identify on the battlefront. An 8m *Kurbelmast* (telescopic mast) fitted with a *Sternantenne* (star antenna) 'a' could be mounted for long-range communications.

Two long-range radios were fitted in racks at the rear left of the fighting compartment: the FuG 12 (80W) had a range of 70km (voice) and 200km (Morse) when using a telescopic mast aerial, and 25km (voice); 80km (Morse) using the standard *Rahmenantenne*. The FuG 19 (15W) transceiver had an effective range of 20km (voice) and 50km (Morse).

The vehicle was armed with an MG 34 and two machine pistols.

The SdKfz 251/7 *Pionier-Gerätewagen* (engineer equipment carrier) was fitted with brackets to carry *Übergansschien* (bridging sections) on each side of the superstructure. The vehicle also carried other specialist equipment, including explosive charges.

The *schwere Wurfgerät* (heavy launching device) 40 could be fitted to all SdKfz 251. A simple aiming device was fitted in front of the driver. The crew has named their carrier *'Wiesel'* (weasel)

SdKfz 251/7

This *mittlerer Pionier-Panzerwagen* (m Pi PzWg) was the vehicle specifically for an armoured engineer battalion in a Panzer division. The vehicle carried a length of an 8,000kg-capacity *Übergangsschiene*(bridging section) on each side of the superstructure. It was armed with two MG 34 and two machine pistols; or two MG 34, a machine pistol and also a PzB 39.

SdKfz 251/8

The *mittlerer Kranken-Panzerwagen* (m KrPzWg – medium armoured ambulance) could carry four casualties on stretchers; more if they could be seated. The vehicle carried two machine pistols.

SdKfz 251/9

Soon after the launch of *Unternehmen* Barbarossa, military planners identified a need for more mobile heavy support weapons. Consequently, the 7.5cm *Sturmkanone* 37 L/24 was mounted on a number of *mittlerer Schützenpanzerwagen* (m SPW – medium armoured personnel carrier) and delivered to front-line units.

Above: The SdKfz 251/8 *Krankenpanzerwagen* (armoured ambulance) was issued to various armoured units. Although painted with prominent red crosses, they were usually armed with two 7.92mm *Maschinenpistole* (MP – machine pistol) 38 or 40.

Left: The SdKfz 251/8 could carry four stretchers or significantly more seated casualties.

Right: The racks for the two stretchers were folded down and supported by vertical bars. Note the water barrel mounted between the front seats.

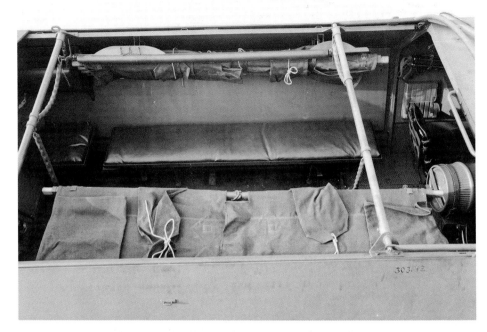

Below: From 1942, the SdKfz 250 began to be issued in larger numbers to the motorcycle rifle battalions. Like the medium carrier, the SdKfz 250/1 was also mounted with two MG 34 machine guns. The vehicle carries the distinctive 'Ghost' symbol of 11.PzDiv.

SdKfz 251/10

On this version the standard MG was removed and replaced with a 3.7cm PaK to provide the platoon leader in a rifle company with a light anti-tank weapon. The crew of six was supplied with an MG 34 and two machine pistols for self defence. A PzB 39 anti-tank rifle was also carried in the vehicle.

SdKfz 251 - *Wurfgerät*

An interesting weapon issued to the *Panzerpionier* battalions and some *Schützen-Kompanien* (rifle companies) was the *schwere Wurfgerät* (heavy missile device) for launching the 28cm *Wurfkörper Spreng* (high-explosive missile) or 32cm *Wurfkörper Flamm* (incendiary missile). Each missile was carried in either wooden or angle-section steel *Packkiste* (storage crate) which would then be mounted on a *Wurfrahmen* (launching frame) before firing.

The launching frame was fitted over the crew compartment of an SdKfz 251, without any modifications, and could carry six *Packkisten*: three

A line of SdKfz 251 Ausf C which were delivered to I./PzGrenRgt 9 in 26.PzDiv when it was being established in France. Some vehicles have a riveted *Panzeraufbau* (armour body), while others have been welded.

Above: The SdKfz 251/10 was armed with a 3.7cm PaK. A support frame had to be fabricated and fitted to carry the extra weight of the weapon.

Right: The SdKfz 250/11 mounted a 2.8cm s PzB 41 and was intended to provide carrier-equipped motorcycle rifle units with a weapon capable of fighting enemy armour. Each anti-tank section was issued with three vehicles.

on each side. In action, the vehicle would be aimed at the target and the elevation, from 16 to 45 degrees, of the *Packkisten* set. The *Wurfkörper Spreng* had an effective range of between 975m and 1,925m; the *Wurfkörper Flamm* was effective from 1,150m to 2,200m.

Leichter Schützenpanzerwagen

Even before production of the light armoured personnel carrier began, two armoured support vehicles were already in service with assault artillery units:

SdKfz 253: *leichter gepanzerter Beobachtungskraftwagen* (le gep BeobKw – light armoured observation vehicle).
SdKfz 252: *leichter gepanzerter Munitionskraftwagen* (le gep MunKw – light armoured ammunition carrier).

These support vehicles were delivered to *Sturmgeschütz* (StuG – assault gun) units to provide respectively artillery observation and ammunition supply under armour protection. Both versions remained in production until 1941.

In November 1940, a list of planned SdKfz 250 variants was published in the *Allgemeine Heeres-Mitteilungen* (general army bulletin).

The 7.5cm KwK L/24 was one of the most important weapons to be mounted on the medium carrier. Designated SdKfz 251/9, the type was usually deployed to provide the PzGren with effective high-explosive supporting fire. In an emergency, the gun could fire shaped-charge ammunition against enemy tanks.

Above: The SdKfz 250/1 carried a *Halbgruppe* (half section) of four men, plus the driver and radio operator. The type mounted two machine guns, which gave it considerable firepower.

Right: This SdKfz 10 chassis, fitted with a dummy superstructure, is possibly the prototype for *Sonderkraftfahrzeug* (SdKfz – special purpose vehicle) 250.

Above: The SdKfz 250 was fitted with the same 4,170cc Maybach TRKM 41 engine as the SdKfz 251, giving the type a better power-to-weight ratio.

Right: The front-axle assembly from the SdKfz 10 was used, unchanged, for the SdKfz 250, proving to be the weakest point of the design.

The layout of the radio equipment in an SdKfz 250/5, was identical to that of the SdKfz 251/3 built in 1943. The conspicuous frame antenna began to be replaced in 1942 by the *Sternantenne* (star antenna).

Two SdKfz 250/5 *Beobachtungswagen* (observation vehicles) in North Africa, both carrying the tactical sign for the artillery regiment in 10.PzDiv. The type was issued both to forward observers and staff echelons.

SdKfz 250/1

The *leichter Schützenpanzerwagen* (le SPW – light armoured personnel carrier) vehicle carried a *Halbgruppe* (half section) of four riflemen, the section commander and the driver. The vehicle was armed with two MG 34 and a machine pistol. One was mounted behind a small *Panzerschild* (armour shield) at the front of the open superstructure, the second was fitted on a pivot-type gun mounting at the rear.

SdKfz 250/2

This *leichter Fernsprech-Panzerwagen* (le FernSprPzWg – armoured telephone or cable layer) carried a telephone section to establish cable phone connections with ten extensions. The vehicle was to have a crew of four, and carried an MG 34, a machine pistol and four 98k rifles. Although listed in November 1940, the type went into production around mid-1942. It is unlikely that great quantities were manufactured.

SdKfz 250/3

This *leichter Funk-Panzerwagen* (le FuPzWg – light armoured radio vehicle) was designed to be fitted with different types of radio equipment. This was carried in racks, inside the fighting compartment, which were designed to allow the equipment to be quickly removed or exchanged.

FuG 8

The FuG 8 (30W transmitter) was the standard radio used by the battalion staff section to keep contact with companies on the battlefront. The equipment had a maximum range of 50km (voice) and 100km (Morse).

FuG 7

This was used by the *Flieger-Verbindungsoffizier* (FliVO – ground-to-air liaison officer).

FuG 12

This radio was used by higher command echelons and had a maximum range of 25km (voice) and 80km (Morse). The FuG 12 (80W transmitter) was only operated with a *Rahmenantenne* (frame antenna).

Far right: An SdKfz 250 leads a column of six SdKfz 251 as German forces advance across the open terrain of western Russia, during *Unternehmen* Barbarossa, towards their ultimate goal: Moscow.

Below: The interior of a SdKfz 251/6 command vehicle: To the right the long-range 100W Sender (S – transmitter) is visible; the corresponding *Tornister* (Torn – backpack [portable]) *Empfänger* (E – receiver) 'b' is mounted to the left. In the middle, mounted one above the other, are a 30W S 'c' and a MW E 'c' (Fu 8).

SdKfz 250/4

The *leichter Luftschutzwagen* (le LuftschPzWg – light armoured air defence vehicle) was developed for front-line units to defend against ground-attack aircraft. The type was fitted with a *Zwillings-Sockellafette* (ZwiSoLa – twin mounting) 36 which was purpose-designed for the *Maschinengewehr* (MG – machine gun) 34. In motorized units the Stöwer light cross-country vehicle was introduced as the Kfz 4, but the versatile ZwiSoLa mounting could be used on almost any type of car or truck. The mounting was even fitted on the wagons of horse-drawn units.

SdKfz 250/5

Military planners decided to replace the SdKfz 253 armoured observation vehicle in service with *Sturmgeschütz* (StuG – assault gun) and artillery units. The replacement vehicle was designated SdKfz 250/5, *leichter Beobachtungspanzerwagen* (le BeobPzWg – light armoured observation

The SdKfz 250/7 mounted
an 8cm *Granatwerfer*
(GrW - grenade launcher
[mortar]) 34. The vehicles
were initially used by the
light SchtzKp (gp) in the
motorcycle rifle battalions.

vehicle), and was equipped with specialized optical equipment, including the *Scherenfernrohr* (SF – scissors-type periscopic sight) and fitted with a FuG 8 radio. An additional FuG 4 was fitted for service with artillery units. The SdKfz 250/5 was also used as a *leichter Aufklärungspanzerwagen* (le AufklPzWg – light armoured reconnaissance vehicle) by the *Panzer-Aufklärungabteilungen* (PzAufklAbt – reconnaissance battalions) in armoured units and fitted with a FuG 12 radio. The type was armed with an MG 34 and carried two machine pistols. From 1942, the SdKfz 250/5 became the standard observation vehicle in artillery and armoured reconnaissance units.

SdKfz 250/6

The *leichter Munitionspanzerwagen* (le MunPzWg – light armoured ammunition carrier) variant was produced to replace the SdKfz 252 ammunition carrier in *Sturmgeschütz* (StuG – assault gun) units. Two versions of the SdKfz 250/6 were produced: the *Ausführung* (Ausf – model/mark) A carried 70 rounds of

Above: The crew of
this SdKfz 250/7 has,
for an unknown reason,
welded non-standard
brackets on the side of the
superstructure.

Right: The SdKfz 250/10
platoon leader's vehicle,
mounted a 3.7cm PaK and
was issued to the SchtzKp
(gp) in a motorcycle rifle
battalion.

7.5cm *Kampfwagenkanone* (KwK – fighting vehicle gun) 37 L/24 ammunition; the Ausf B carried 60 rounds of 7.5cm KwK 40 L/43 ammunition.

SdKfz 250/7

This *leichter Schützenpanzerwagen* (GrW) version carried an 8cm *schwere Geratwerfer* (s GrW – heavy grenade launcher [mortar]) 34 plus a crew of eight. The mortar could be fired from inside the vehicle, but a standard *Bodenplatte* (base plate) was also carried so that the weapon could be dismounted. The vehicle was armed with an MG 34 and carried a machine pistol.

Identification

The purpose of each variant was identifiable by the addition of a numeral to the type designation: SdKfz 251/1, SdKfz 251/2 or SdKfz 250/1, 250/2 etc. Any alteration to the basic specification was indicated by changing the *Ausführung* (Ausf – model/mark).

SdKfz 251 (Unarmoured)

A small series of medium personnel carriers were fabricated using *Weicheisen* (mild steel). Visually, these vehicles are identical to the armoured version.

An SdKfz 250 in service with 1.SS-PzDiv Leibstandarte Adolf Hitler. A line of *Selbstsfahrlafette* (Sfl – self-propelled) anti-tank guns from the divisional PzJgAbt, including a 7.5cm PaK 40 auf PzKpfw 38 (*Marder* [marten] III) Ausf H, are in the background.

Above: The *Panzerschild* (armour shield) fitted for the MG 34 only gave the gunner minimal protection from infantry weapons.

Right: The *schwere Maschinengewehr Lafette* (heavy machine-gun carriage) 34 could be mounted in both the SdKfz 250 and SdKfz 251 to allow long bursts of accurate fire to be directed at a target. The carriage was fitted with a *Zielfernrohr* (ZF – periscopic sight) 12 to keep the gunner protected.

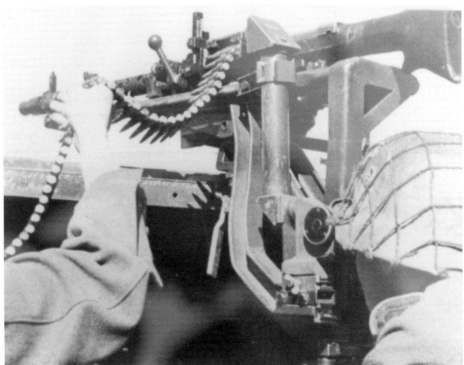

These track links must have been temporarily placed in front of the *Panzerschild*, since they would impede the MG 34.

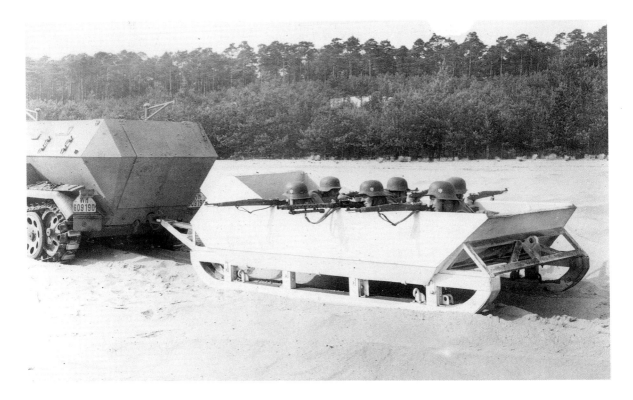

In winter the Russians used sledges to transport infantry and this inspired the Germans to develop a *Anhängeschlitten für Panzer* (sledge towed by armoured vehicles). However, this image was taken in the summer of 1942 during trials over sandy terrain; an attempt to simulate soft snow.

SdKfz 251 Ausf A

The bodywork for the *Ausführung* (Ausf – version/model) A was fabricated from armoured steel plates which gave protection from 7.92mm *Spitzgeschoss mit Kern* (SmK – armour-piercing ammunition).

SdKfz 251 Ausf B

The only way to differentiate an Ausf A from an Ausf B is that the number of vision apertures on each side of the superstructure was reduced from three to one.

SdKfz 251 Ausf C

In 1941, the superstructure for the Ausf C was virtually redesigned to address a number of weak points. For example, the air vents on the engine cover were altered to improve cooling and protection. Interestingly, one of the subcontractors produced an unknown quantity of Ausf C with riveted construction.

SdKfz 251 Ausf D

In mid-1943 the shape of the superstructure was fundamentally revised; a one-piece door was fitted in the rear plate and the side armour was significantly simplified. The hinged visors were removed and the apertures fitted with bullet-proof glass blocks.

SdKfz 250

When the type first entered service, it was almost impossible to differentiate it from an SdKfz 253. In profile they were almost identical, but the latter had a fully enclosed superstructure. Those first SdKfz 250 were designated Ausf A until the SdKfz 250 Ausf B entered production.

SdKfz 250 Ausf B

In 1942, the superstructure was redesigned to simplify production by reducing the number of plates required and eliminating labour-intensive work. The number of engine access hatches was reduced from three to one and all hinged visors were removed and the apertures fitted with bullet-proof glass vision blocks.

The difference between variants was not important to the troops on the battlefront, nor was it to the maintenance services since they were mechanically identical.

In early 1943, the MG 42 began to gradually replace the MG 34. The new weapon had a significantly increased rate of fire and was more reliable, being built using pressed metal components. Also, its design was simpler, making it cheaper to produce.

Above: The SdKfz 251 Ausf C was fitted with a redesigned *Panzeraufbau* (armour body). The *Frontpanzer* (front armour) was simplified, while at the same time improving armour protection.

Right: This SdKfz 251/6 was issued for use by a *Fliegerverbindungsoffizier* (ground-to-air liaison officer) from the *Luftwaffe*. A 1.4m rod antenna has been fitted for a Fu 7, long-range radio, and the frame antenna indicates that the vehicle also carries a Fu 12.

Above: The SdKfz 251/10 mounting a 3.7cm PaK first entered service in mid-1941. When mounted on an SdKfz 251 Ausf C, the gun was fitted with a smaller double gun shield which protected only the gunner.

Left: An SdKfz 251/1 being used for driver training, which would be carried out by the replacement units. But circumstances often caused driver instruction to be conducted in the vicinity of front-line positions.

7

1942 – ARMOURED INFANTRY

After the failure of *Unternehmen* Taifun (Operation *Typhoon*) at Moscow, the ambitious goals of the *Unternehmen* Barbarossa could no longer be achieved. On the contrary, the Red Army had achieved a significant success in stopping the German invaders.

The Panzer divisions were in poor condition; all vehicles, especially tanks and armoured personnel carriers, had been affected by months of mechanical wear. In addition, the overstretched supply routes led to considerable difficulties with replacement vehicles, spare parts and the delivery of sufficient fuel. The crisis feared by German commanders could no longer be averted.

The severe weather conditions of the Russian winter forced Heeresgruppe Mitte (Army Group Centre) to go on the defensive, but due to the high number of vehicles lost the riflemen now had to fight on foot; often from fox hole to fox hole or trench to trench just to hold territory gained in the battle for Moscow.

SdKfz 250

By the end of 1941, the monthly production rate of the SdKfz 251 and Sdkfz 250 armoured personnel carriers had reached an average of 70 each.

The original plan was for the production of the SdKfz 250 *leichter Schützenpanzerwagen* (le SPW – light armoured personnel carrier) to commence in 1939, but due to constantly changing circumstances – the lack of materials and production capacity – it was postponed several times.

On 21 January 1942, the *Organisations-Abteilung* (OrgAbt – organization department) reported in its war diary:

> The SdKfz 250, which is about to enter production should, in the first instance, be issued to the rifle units of the *Schnelle-Truppen* [rapid forces] in conjunction with the SdKfz 251. The

Summer 1942: Two SdKfz 251, followed by an SdKfz 250/3 from Heeresgruppe Süd (Army Group South); both are painted in standard *dunkelgrau* (dark grey) but their crews have applied mud in a camouflage pattern.

Right: Winter conditions in Russia affected all types of German tracked vehicle. Here, snow has piled up in front of an SdKfz 251, which would restrict steering movements and severely stress the component parts.

Below: An early production SdKfz 251/10: The height of the tarpaulin indicates that the 3.7cm PaK is fitted with the original high gun shield.

original plans cannot be implemented, since the numbers of SdKfz 251 necessary to equip entire rifle battalions and regiments will not be available in the foreseeable future. In order to make best use of the new SdKfz 250, it is proposed to use them to enhance the combat capabilities of the motorcycle rifle units. Meanwhile, an order has been issued to all army groups for those armoured personnel carriers that reach the front to be delivered only to the combat units (not staff companies).

Armoured personnel carriers in service with Panzer-Lehr-Regiment 901. This instructional unit was deployed to southern Russia in 1942. The 3.7cm PaK on this SdKfz 251/10 is fitted with the later type of gun shield. The soldier in front of the gun carries a Russian 7.62mm Tokarev SVT-40 semi-automatic rifle; German designation *Selbstladegewehr* 259(r).

Organizational Changes

Quite understandably, military planners gave priority to delivering those available le SPW and m SPW to combat units, but officers at higher command levels and their signals units were also issued with armoured personnel carriers. While the soon-to-be-renamed rifle battalions were at first dependent on the SdKfz 251, all the staff sections, despite the reservations issued by the OrgAbt, also received the Sdkfz 250.

In early 1942, orders were issued for a clear demarcation between the rifle regiments in the rifle brigade and the *Kradschützen* (KradSchtz – motorcycle rifle) battalion, so that they could be amalgamated with the *Panzeraufklärungs-Abteilung* (PzAufklAbt – armoured reconnaissance

PzGren in snow-covered terrain: All are wearing *Winter-Wendeuniform* (reversable winter uniform); one side was white and the other had *Splittertarnmuster* (splinter-pattern camouflage).

battalion), to form a significantly more effective combat force. The subunit was temporarily designated as a *Kradschützen-Bataillon* (KradSchtz-Btl – motor cycle rifle battalion).

Although the majority of SdKfz 250 would be issued to the new KradSchtz-Btl – later PzAufklAbt – substantial numbers were being delivered to the *Panzerartillerie* regiments in Panzer divisions.

In early 1942, the existing Panzer division structures were in the process of being adapted to meet new operations. Planning for the offensive in southern Russia, *Fall Blau* (Case Blue), had been completed and the participating Panzer divisions were undergoing heavy maintenance or the process of being re-equipped. Their rifle units were being mechanized, but the allocation of vehicles and of which type is impossible due to a lack of accurate information in the relevant KStN structures. However, it is almost certain that if armoured personnel carriers were unavailable, then units would receive soft-skinned vehicles.

SchtzRgt and SchtzBtl in 1942

The spring of 1942 saw a gradual improvement in the supply of replacement equipment and personnel to those tank divisions deployed on the Russian battlefront. Improved production finally made it possible to equip at least one battalion in each tank division with armoured personnel carriers.

The standard rifle brigade still consisted of two regiments, each having two battalions. But only one of the four battalions was armoured (gp), the remaining three were *motorisiert* (motorized) units, due to an insufficient number of MTW/SPW being manufactured. At regimental level, a *Stabskompanie* (staff company) consisting of a signals platoon, an anti-tank platoon and a motor-cycle rifle platoon, for reconnaissance duties, was added.

The tracks fitted on all types of German *Halbkettenfahrzeug* (half-track motor vehicle) required constant maintenance; cleaning and lubrication was daily requirement.

Above: A number of battle-damaged SdKfz 251 carriers have been loaded on railway wagons to be transported to workshop units where they will be refurbished.

Right: Despite the fact that the anti-tank ballistics of the 3.7cm PaK were obsolete by 1943, it became an effective support weapon when high-explosive ammunition was made available.

Above: An *Oberfeldwebel* among the ruins of the battle-torn city of Stalingrad. His helmet is fitted with a *Splittertarn* (splinter-pattern camouflage) cover and he is armed with a Russian 7.62mm PPSh submachine gun.

Left: An SdKfz 251/1 Ausf C of 16.PzDiv leads a column of armoured personnel carriers during the Battle of Stalingrad [now Volgograd], which began on 23 August 1942 and ended on 2 February 1943.

The SdKfz 251/10 was deployed as platoon leader's vehicle in PzGrenKp 'c'. The vehicle carried 168 rounds of 3.7cm anti-tank ammunition.

SchtzBtl (mot)

The original *Schützen-Bataillon* (SchtzBtl – rifle battalion) had three motorized rifle companies and a heavy company. Each company was now authorized to have three 7.92mm *Panzerbüchse* (PzB – anti-tank rifle) 39; although these were considered to be obsolete by 1942 standards. The anti-tank platoon was significantly strengthened when the 3.7cm *Panzerabwehrkanone* (PaK – anti-tank gun) was replaced by the more effective 5cm PaK 38.

The removal of the motorcycle rifle battalion would have left the rifle regiment without an effective reconnaissance and as a result every rifle battalion staff received a motorcycle platoon.

The strong machine-gun company had been dropped, but this was more than balanced by increasing the number of machine guns in the three rifle platoons. The 8cm *schwere Granatwerfer* (s GrW – heavy grenade launcher [mortar]) 34 was now integrated into the heavy companies of the rifle divisions.

SchtzBtl (gp)

On the staff levels, small numbers of SdKfz 250/3 and SdKfz 250/2 were

assigned to provide the higher echelons with armoured command and communications vehicles.

The *gepanzertes Schützen-Bataillon* (SchtzBtl [gp] – rifle battalion [armoured]) was organized according the latest structures dated 1 November 1941:

Stab eines Schützen-Bataillon (gp), to KStN 1108 (gp)
Schützen-Kompanie (gp), to KStN 1141
Schwere Kompanie (heavy company)
Gruppe Führer (staff section), to KStN 1121 (gp)
Panzerjäger-Zug, three 5cm PaK 38, to KStN 1122a (gp)
schwere Panzerbüchse-Zug, three 2.8cm s PzB 41
Infanteriegeschütz-Zug, two 7.5cm le IG 18, to KStN 1123 (gp)
Pionier-Zug, to KStN 1124 (gp)

From mid-1942, the title '*Panzergrenadier*' was to become generally accepted, both for the individual soldier and also for the units in what had been the rifle brigades.

This SdKfz 251/10 Ausf C, armed with a 3.7cm PaK, is in service with 23.PzDiv. Formed in France in late 1941, the division adopted an *Eiffelturm* (a stylized Eiffel Tower) as its emblem.

The PzGrenBrig of 9.PzDiv in summer 1942.

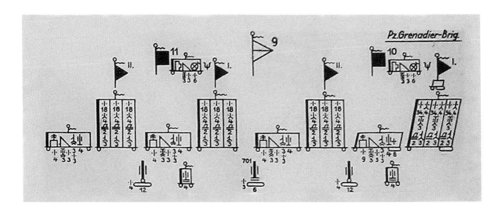

Schützen-Kompanie b (gp) (KStN 1114)

SchtzRgt 1, 1.PzDiv on 1 November 1941

Kp Trupp	1. Zug	2. Zug	3. Zug	schwerer Zug	Gefechts-Tross	Gepäck-Tross	Hilfs-Trupp
SdKfz 250/3	SdKfz 251/10 3,7 cm	SdKfz 251/10 3,7 cm	SdKfz 251/10 3,7 cm	SdKfz 251/1	Kfz 15	⌃	⌃
SdKfz 250/3	⌃	⌃	⌃	⌃	⌃	le gl Lkw	le gl Lkw
⌃	SdKfz 251/1	SdKfz 251/1	SdKfz 251/1	SdKfz 251/1	le gl Lkw		
↑	SdKfz 251/1	SdKfz 251/1	SdKfz 251/1	SdKfz 251/1	le gl Lkw		
↑	SdKfz 251/1	SdKfz 251/1	SdKfz 251/1	SdKfz 251/2 8 cm	le gl Lkw		
↑				SdKfz 251/2 8 cm	le gl Lkw		

Subsequently, the designation *Panzergrenadierwagen* (PGW) was sometimes used instead of *Schützenpanzerwagen* (SPW), but the latter was more commonly used up until end of the war.

Motorcycle Battalion

The *Kradschützen* battalion now consisted of the *Bataillons-Stab* (battalion staff), two *Kradschützen-Kompanien*, one *leichte Schützen-Kompanie* (gep), a *schwere Kompanie*, a *Panzerspähwagen-Kompanie* (PzSpWgKp – armoured car company) and also a supply column. The unit would gradually be re-equipped for armoured reconnaissance duties.

Schwere Kompanie (gp) (KStN 1121)
SchtzRgt 10, 9.PzDiv in summer 1942

Kp Trupp	Geschütz Zug	Pionier Zug	Panzerjäger Zug		Gefechts-Tross**	Gepäck-Tross**	Hilfs-Trupp**
SdKfz 250/3	SdKfz 250/1	SdKfz 250/1	SdKfz 251/1		Kfz 15	↑	↑
SdKfz 250/2	↑	↑	↑	↑	↑	le gl Lkw	le gl Lkw
↑	SdKfz 251/3 7,5	SdKfz 251/5	SdKfz 251/3 7,5*	SdKfz 251/3 7,5*	le gl Lkw		
↑	SdKfz 251/3 7,5	SdKfz 251/5	SdKfz 251/4 7,5*		le gl Lkw		
↑	SdKfz 251/4 Mun	SdKfz 251/5			le gl Lkw		
↑		SdKfz 251/5	SdKfz 251/4 Mun	SdKfz 251/4 Mun	le gl Lkw		
		SdKfz 251/5					

After a winter of fighting, 3.PzDiv – although seriously depleted – was deployed with various *Kampfgruppen* fighting on the Kursk salient. These battle groups were often assembled in a random fashion, with elements taken from what remained of subunits. Since the division was selected to participate in *Fall Blau* (Case Blue), the invasion of the Caucasus, an order was issued on 3 June 1942 for its *Auffrischung* (replenishment) in the field.

The replenishment did not go to plan; the necessary troops and equipment were delivered, but not the required number of vehicles, including *Zugkraftwagen* (tractors), which would severely restrict mobility.

On 27 May 1942, 3.PzDiv delivered the following strength report to the command echelon of VIII.Armeekorps (AK – Army Corps):

a.) Tank situation PzRgt 6

Combat ready:

13 PzKpfw II, 29 PzKpfw III kurz, 18 PzKpfw III lang, 14 PzKpfw IV kurz, 12 PzKpfw IV lang (less two because trained crews are lacking)

PzJgAbt 521 (attached from army level)

12 Sfl 7.62cm PaK, Four Sfl 4.7cm PaK

[Note: *Kurzrohr* (kurz – short barrel): *Langrohr* (lang – long barrel)]

b.) *Schützenregimenter*:

Mobility:

One Btl of SchtzRgt 3 on SPW with 2½ Kp combat ready. KradSchtzBtl III with one SPW Kp and one PzSpKp (only the SPW Kp is fully mobile with supply vehicles).

1386006

A PzGrenBtl (gp) formation advances across the vast open Steppe – flat, unforested grassland – of southern Russia. The heavy company [left] is equipped with six SdKfz 251/9 *Kanonenwagen* armed with the 7.5cm *Sturmkanone* (StuK – assault gun) 37 L/24.

An SdKfz 250/3 of the *Nachrichtenzug* (signals platoon) from a motorcycle rifle battalion. Note the SdKfz 10 tractors towing 7.5cm *schwere Panzerabwehrkanone* (s PaK – heavy anti-tank guns) 97/38 of the PzJg elements. (Ullstein via Getty)

A group of PzGren, all wearing *Winter-Wendeuniform* (reversible winter uniform), use the hulk of an enemy tank, here a T-34/76, as a temporary bunker. To the left, a 7.92mm *Panzerbüchse* (PzB – anti-tank rifle) 39 has been leant against the tank.

Immobile:

Three SchtzBtl on foot, with normal weapons and equipment. All heavy weapons are immobile.

Two Kp KradSchtzBtl are immobile and without supply vehicles.

c.) Artillery

Combat ready:

One light battalion with three batteries, of which two are mobile with tractors – provided that the delivery is made by 1 June. One battery equipped with *Beute-Traktoren* [captured tractors] is mobile. Supply trucks are available only for one battery.

One FlaK battalion with two heavy and one light battery are fully operational.

The rest of the artillery (one light battalion and the heavy battalion) are immobile.

c.) PzJgAbt (divisional tank destroyer battalion)

The battalion is not operational, since all Unic tractors [French-built vehicles] were delivered without towing hooks.

d.) *Pionier-Battalion*

One Kp (SPW) is fully operational. Two companies are immobile and also lack supply vehicles. The *Brückenleger-Kompanie* [BrüKp – bridge-laying company] 'K' is immobile without supply vehicles.

f.) *Nachrichten-Abteilung*

To effectively lead the division, the allocation of the following to the signals sections is absolutely necessary:

One *Fernsprechbetriebstrupp* 'a' (mot)

Six *grosse Fernsprechtrupps* 'a' (mot)

Five *kleine Fernsprechbetriebstrupps* (mot)

15 *mittle Funktrupps* 'b' (mot) 80W

One *le Nachrichten-Kolonne* (supply column)

New vehicles for both signals columns.

g.) Transport columns

The available transport capacity (supply) is only sufficient for a *kleine Kampfgruppe* [small combat group] consisting of a *verstärkte Panzer-Abteilung* [reinforced tank battalion].

A two-man 8cm *Granatwerfer* (GrW – grenade launcher [mortar]) team accompany a Pioneer carrying a portable *Flammenwerfer* (FmW – flame thrower) 41 and also a *Pistole* P 38.

Despite the planned replenishment, the situation in 3.PzDiv remained desperate since the unit still lacked some 70 percent of the supply trucks and tractors required. The artillery regiment was without mobile heavy weapons (10cm s K 18 and 15cm s FH 18) and the PzJgAbt was not operational

Far left: A platoon of PzGren armed with K 98k rifles and supported by two MG 34 teams, take up a defensive position in a roadside ditch during the advance through Latvia in 1941.

Left: By 1942 most German armoured carriers, including the SdKfz 251, had been fitted with a FuSprech 'f' transceiver. This vehicle has an additional antenna, possibly due to it having a *TornisterFunkgeräte* (TornFuG – backpack [portable] transceiver).

Below: Stalingrad: A three-man heavy MG team trudge through the debris of an industrial site. The soldier carries a *schwere Machinengewehr Lafette* (heavy machine-gun carriage) on his back.

Above: An SdKfz 251/1 Ausf B in service with 23.PzDiv. The crew has opened both vision apertures and also removed the bullet-proof glass blocks to improve observation.

Right: The SdKfz 251/3 *Funkwagen* (radio vehicle), which entered service in 1943, was supplied in five different versions. The Typ III carried a FuG 7 VHF transceiver to allow a *Luftwaffe* liaison officer have ground-to-air communications with patrolling aircraft. Note the aircraft-type MG 15, fitted with a *Patronentrommel* (saddle drum magazine).

because the French-built tractors had been supplied without suitable towing hooks.

The target for the number of tanks and armoured personnel carriers delivered seems to have been reached, although only one *Schützen* battalion received a full complement of armoured carriers. A further document reports that the division received nine 3.7cm PaK-armed SdKfz 251/10 and another SdKfz 251/10 *Zugführerwagen* (platoon leader's vehicle) for each platoon.

On 6 June 1942, I./SchtzRg 126 (26.PzDiv) submitted an extensive after-action report:

Experience report on combat by the battalion from 12 May to 28 May at the northern and southern front at Kharkov.

A: Tactical Commitment.

Structure of the battalion during the fighting
The battalion was almost entirely part of the battle groups fighting at focal points on the front. Further elements of the battle group were committed by the Panzer regiment: an artillery battalion; a *Panzerjäger* company; an armoured *Pionier* section; and a forward medical clearing station. All elements were under command of the *Schützen* brigade's staff.
Tactical Missions.
During the attack the battalion was committed as 2.Kp, with parts of 3.Kp following the Panzer regiment. Therefore, the force was more like a light tank division than a rifle battalion. Due to the difficult terrain and enemy fire, the unarmoured parts of the battalion often had to be left behind, especially the heavy company. For this reason, we consider it absolutely essential to keep the heavy company in the *Schützen* battalion under armour protection. When encountering enemy tanks, the armoured halftracks must be kept a safe distant behind our tanks. They should follow using rapid and decisive moves by using all available cover. Reason: the tanks attract fire from heavy weapons and anti-tank guns. While our tanks are less vulnerable, the thinly armoured carriers are at risk. Since the enemy normally concentrates its anti-tank weapons, a tank company designated the sole task of attacking and destroying them is absolutely necessary for the success of a larger operation.
Marching
When *Schützen-Kompanien* (gp) are moving towards their assembly areas, strict traffic regulation, enforced by *Feld-Gendarmerie* [military police], is absolutely necessary. These routes have to be clearly marked during hours of darkness. During the march from Krutojarka to Kharkov, it again proved wrong to let tracked columns march with wheeled columns following. Even in light rain, road surfaces were churned up by the

tracked vehicles, which made it impossible for supply trucks to get through. As a result, the final elements of the SchtzBtl reached Merefa some 31 hours late.

Communications

Within the battle groups reliable radio communications is required between all commanders or independent company commanders. The battalion command post maintained radio communication with the company commanders by means of a 30W Sender, the *Funksprech* 'a' was used to keep in contact with individual armoured carriers. The initial uncertainty in radio communication was due to the limited training received by our radio operators, but this has now been now resolved. Radio communications within the battalion has proved to be successful. In future, radio documents must not be assigned to SchtzRgt 126, because it was not tactically attached during the operation, but must be handed directly to the battalion.

The Attack

Before the start of the attack, at least 30 minutes are required to brief all company, platoon and group commanders. Sufficient time must also be allowed for combat reconnaissance.

Care of the wounded

The rifle battalion requires at least one *Kranken-Panzerwagen* [SdKfz 251/8]. During the operation, our medics were assigned a standard armoured personnel carrier to evacuate the wounded from the battlefield. Although a *Sanka* [wheeled ambulance] was available it was not used during the operation.

Our Troops

The battalion performed very well in all situations; no enemy tanks penetrated our lines.

General Issues

Occasionally superior command echelons issued orders for armoured half-track vehicles in the battalion to be deployed for transporting ammunition and rations. This meant that weapons, equipment and ammunition had to be unloaded and stored under guard. Consequently, the combat strength of the battalion was significantly, although temporarily, weakened.

B. Equipment and Supply

Material equipment

The Kfz 2/40 is not a suitable vehicle for the workshop unit of an armoured half-track company; it is too small and easily overloaded. We would suggest a SdKfz 10 instead. The required number of hand grenades (stick and egg types) must be doubled. Each vehicle should carry at least two smoke grenades to cover a retreat in open terrain when attacked by enemy anti-tank guns. The number of signal flares, especially white, is not sufficient for *Grosskampftage* [great battles]. The heavy company requires twelve troopers to carry rations as opposed to the six at present; this is considered essential since the heavy company often becomes dispersed during a battle.

SdKfz 250 and SdKfz 251

Both types of armoured personnel carrier have performed extraordinarily well and have adequate armour protection and speed. In most instances the workshop is only required to repair broken front axles, spring eyes and sheared-off bolts. But the front leaf springs are too weak and the armoured engine cover makes any repair or maintenance work unnecessarily difficult. Off road, the vehicle bounces too much, which must be addressed. The rear access doors were never really needed; the internal hinges take up precious space. We suggest for future developments to drop the rear doors completely. The steering brakes frequently have to be adjusted, but they are very difficult to access.

The operation of the handbrake is problematic. If the driver moves with the handbrake applied, the transmission brake wedges will shear off, resulting in the vehicle being out of service for a lengthy period.

Two SdKfz 251/1 Ausf C from an unidentified PzGren unit move through scrub-covered terrain in the Caucasus. Both vehicles have a rear-mounted MG 42 which suggests that this image was taken in 1943.

The glass lenses of the headlights on the SdKfz 250/10 are frequently shattered by the muzzle blast of the 3.7cm PaK.

All SdKfz 251 must be fitted with a towing hook suitable for the 5cm PaK 38 and the 7.5cm le IG 18.

Radio Equipment

The *Funksprech* (FuSpr – transceiver) 'a' has proven to be effective, but the voice reproduction is sometimes distorted. The supply of spare parts for the transceiver is insufficient.

The *Funkgerät* 8 (FuG – radio device)

The *Rahmenantenne* (frame-type antenna) must be replaced: it is conspicuous and easily identifies the halftrack as a command vehicle. The antenna also makes it impossible to use the rear *Machinengewehr* (MG – machine gun) 34 swivel-arm mounting for anti-aircraft defence. Also, in two instances, a hand grenade thrown from inside the vehicle has struck the antenna and dropped back into the troop compartment.

Weapons and Associated Equipment

The 7.92mm MG 34 machine gun has proven to be reliable and provided excellent firepower for the battalion. The special *schwere Machinengewehr Lafette* [heavy machine

gun carriage] 34 is good, and is preferred to the *Panzerschild* [armour shield] mounting. Suggestion: instead of the belt-fed ammunition, which frequently jams, a new type, based on that used for the MG in our tanks, should be introduced with some urgency. Mounting a 3.7cm PaK on both types of armoured halftrack has proven to be very successful, but due to the construction of the gun, the *Zielfernrohr* [ZF – sighting telescope] cannot be completely pushed into its holder. No experience reports have been received regarding SdKfz 251/2 mounting the 8cm heavy grenade launcher [mortar]. The rifle carrying racks inside the halftrack can be removed to create more storage and baggage space. Holders to carry *Stielhandgranate* (stick hand grenades) must be given priority. Also, it is suggested that a speaking tube be installed as a simple way for the commander to pass instructions to his driver. The holding racks of the *schwere Wurfkörper* [heavy missile] should be designed to be removable so that no damage occurs during the march.

Ammunition

In general, the ammunition consumption during combat could always be replenished. The ammunition for the *schwere Wurfgerät* was transported on [captured] Peugeot light trucks, but this caused major problems. For this reason, the *schwere Wurfgerät* could never be used effectively on the battlefront – off-road-capable transport vehicles are a

Two SdKfz 251/1 fitted with *schwere Wurfgerät* 40. During a longer march, the *Packkisten* (carrying crates), containing the rocket missiles, were transported in trucks.

Above: Adverse weather exacerbated by the condition of many roads in Russia, and the constant shortage of recovery vehicles, meant that any available half-track vehicle had to be used, as with this SdKfz 251.

Right: Manufactured in Stettin by Stöwer Werke, the *Kraftfahrzeug* (Kfz – motor vehicle) 1 was the first standardized light cross-country vehicle. It was later superseded by the VW Typ 82 *Kübelwagen* ('bucket car').

necessity. The proportion of high-explosive rounds in the initial ammunition stock for both 3.7cm PaK and 5cm PaK must be increased. The 3.7cm stick grenades had not been delivered.

Supply

The command transmission between the battalion and combat trains I and II caused problems. This was aggravated by enemy artillery fire and air raids. Despite this, the battalion never suffered from fuel or ammunition shortages.

Spare parts:

The stockpiling of spare parts, in particular those for the armoured halftracks, must be given the greatest attention. As soon as the few spare parts available to the troops are used up, a considerable number of SPW will fail. In case of failure of pneumatic tires, no replacement is available.

After the battle for Kharkov, 3.PzDiv submitted an after-action report, dated 11 June 1942:

Combat experiences of 3.PzDiv, with emphasis on Panzer

General experiences:

The Russian infantry is poorly led and they would not attack without tank support.

The enemy always attacked in packs. Despite the fact that these attacks were always repulsed, more were repeated in the same form with the same result.

If the enemy is attacked, however, the Russian infantry defends bravely to the last man. The Russian soldier is indoctrinated by a political commissar to believe that us Germans never take prisoners. This assumption is partly justified after the winter fighting, when our troops acted in this way. This was propagated by enemy agents and also by the local population. All services emphasize that the troops have to be instructed again and again about the decent treatment of prisoners. It has to be realized that the enemy will eventually be made aware that we are treating prisoners more humanely. Hopefully, we will see a decrease in the reluctance of the Russian infantryman to surrender.

It is advisable to build up reserves. The battle of the division must take place in two combat groups, each group must be accompanied by a rifle regiment. This means that the division still has a motorcycle rifle battalion at its disposal as a mobile reserve.

3.PzDiv had only one SPW company. It is hoped that a further one can be established soon when the vehicles currently being repaired in Krakau return to the division.

Our *Kradschützen* were used for flank cover and reconnaissance. Parts of the battalion formed the divisional riflemen reserve. When possible, the *Panzerspähwagen-Schwadron* [armoured car squadron] had to stay with the riflemen. There is no particular experience with the Kradschtz-Btl in the current new organizational structure, as this was only recently introduced. It is considered appropriate to issue a *FlaK-Kompanie* [Fla-Kp – anti-aircraft company] to the

An SdKfz 251 fitted with a *schwere Wurfgerät* (launching frame) 40 bellowing clouds of dense smoke; it can only be assumed that a smoke candle had been inadvertently ignited.

rifle brigade.

There is no special combat experience with SPW companies, as the division has only one available. It has been observed that this company tended to fight from their vehicles; they are reluctant to leave them for dismounted combat. On several occasions the SPW company requested infantry to support them even though they were completely able to fight the enemy dismounted.

It is important that *Schützen* and Panzer performing the same combat mission use the same medium wave frequencies, so that both can hear all radio messages.

When sending out reconnaissance patrols by *Panzerspähtruppen* [armoured car squads], tracked vehicles should not be used regularly due to the high wear and tear. However, this cannot always be ruled out, as only SPW are equipped with 30W medium wave units. VHF radios do not have the necessary range for reconnaissance units.

Birth of the *Panzergrenadiere*

On 5 July 1942, the Generalstab des Heeres (GenStb d H – General Staff of the Army) issued an order for the rifle brigades and regiments to be reorganized as *Panzergrenadier-Brigaden* (PzGrenBrig) and *Panzergrenadier-Regimenter* (PzGrenRgt) with the men in both known as *Panzergrenadiere* (PzGren).

A short time later, the *Ausbildungsabteilung* (II) (AA – training department) of the GenStb d H issued a directive on the deployment of Panzer and PzGren in 'modern' warfare. The directive was later printed and widely distributed:

Operations in the East

Experiences of Panzer and PzGren units on the attack and in defence during the battle around Kharkov are worthy of attention. Since these are based on reports from individual tank divisions, a final evaluation, which will result in general combat and training instructions being changed, has not yet been made. (The following remarks should be considered only as suggestions).

General issues

Even on fronts where the Russians had tank units in the strength of one or even more brigades, these were never used in concentrated formations on the battlefield. His armoured units usually fought in groups of 20 or 30, and never approached closer than some 2,000m: it was obvious they lacked any leadership. If Russian tank units attacked, they soon split into smaller groups and the fighting force dispersed.

Experiences in the deployment of PzGren on SPW:

a) The SPW battalion will in principle be deployed, even if there is only one battalion, as a cohesive unit that must not become fragmented. Importantly, no individual vehicles must be used for the transport of ammunition, provisions or wounded.

b) Only when the SPW battalion is in close support of the Panzer unit will its combat strength be fully effective. The SPW-mounted PzGren following the tank units also provide

The Caucasus: In July 1942 PzRgt 204, attached to 22.PzDiv, was still equipped with 114 PzKpfw 38(t) as its main armoured element. In the background is a line of SdKfz 251 from of I./PzGrenRgt 129.

protection against close-quarters attack by enemy tank destroyer teams. Additionally, they give our tank crews a sense of security.

c) When our Panzers encounter enemy tanks, then the SPW must be withdrawn to avoid unnecessary exposure to enemy armour-piercing weapons.

d) A constant and sharp observation of the battlefield helps to reduce the effect of enemy anti-tank weapons. Early detection is vital so that they can be attacked and eliminated. Our SPW must attack in force and at high speed to destroy the enemy.

The light SPW company of the newly structured rifle battalions is the strongest infantry force in these units. The company has proven itself in all situations; it is highly mobile and very fast over any terrain. The following experiences have been gathered during the attack:

a) In principle, the company is to be deployed as a closed unit during an attack: no individual SPW are to be diverted for reconnaissance purposes.

b) As long as the terrain allows, the PzGren on le SPW will attack at the head of the

A large two-piece hatch allowed limited access to the engine. To replace the unit, or to replace a component, the complete armoured engine cover had to be removed.

Kradschützen in order to effectively break enemy resistance. Since the *Kradschützen* have to dismount earlier than the PzGren in SPW, time and effort are saved.

c) Also they must be equipped from the outset with sufficient heavy weapons, especially PaK. This will enable the PzGren to effectively combat their most dangerous foe - enemy tanks. When the PzGren dismount, their vehicles must be moved to a safe place and, preferably, protected by anti-tank guns.

In combat, troops travelling in an SdKfz 251 dismounted simply by leaping over the sides of the vehicle.

The Caucasus

On 28 June 1942, German forces launched *Fall Blau* (Case Blue), the strategic summer offensive in southern Russia, to capture the oilfields at Baku and deny the Soviets access to a vital commodity: crude oil. Hitler demanded success, since he envisaged the Red Army running out of fuel and replacement equipment, followed by the collapse of the Soviet Union.

But German forces were short of equipment. Shortages of materials and the lack of production facilities – Allied bombing of strategic targets on Germany had increased in intensity – meant that the supply of armoured half-track

The SdKfz 251/7 (armoured engineer carrier) was identifiable by virtue of the bridging section mounted on each side of the *Panzeraufbau* (armour body). It carried a crew of eight and specialist equipment including explosives.

carriers was not sufficient to meet the demands of front-line units. Only one in four of the PzGrenBtl in a brigade could be issued with the precious carriers. The situation was further complicated by the fact that the armoured rifle battalion had neither time nor resources to train the armoured infantry for mass deployment with the new vehicles.

In combat, the carriers were at first only deployed against the focal point of an attack. But with growing experience and confidence in their equipment, the PzGren became a vital element now able to keep pace with the fast-moving Panzer divisions. Also, as noted in a wartime document, field commanders reported that those units supplied with armoured carriers lost fewer personnel.

On 14 September 1942, *Unteroffizier* Hänle of 2./PzGrenRgt 304 (see 2.PzDiv) submitted his personal report on the fighting at Rzhev (Heeresgruppe Mitte).

Counterattack with SPW during a Russian assault on Ryabinky

9 August 1942. The sun is already far in the west. A dispatch rider delivers the order to get ready. Of course, he is asked what is about to happen, but he only replies, 'It stinks'. We experienced war veterans are quickly ready for action. The platoon leader gives his orders concisely. Our

column leaves its position in a hollow overgrown with bushes and advance over open fields. After 600m we take cover and immediately dig in. We watch the edge of the forest in front of us very closely. After a short time, we hear the sound of engines; our armoured personnel carriers are approaching.

In front of us, to the left, II.Btl is coming under increasingly fierce fire. The SPW are now coming directly towards our positions, we can see the MG gunners behind their armoured shields. We follow the advancing vehicles, when their machine guns suddenly cover the edge of the forest with heavy fire. A 3.7cm *PaK-Wagen* [SdKfz 251/10] fires, and explosive grenades are being thrown. The Russians return fire and a fierce battle begins. A muzzle flash is observed near a tree stump, and then we hear a loud, sharp 'crack'; this can only be an anti-tank gun or rifle. Also, on the right we sight what is obviously an enemy anti-tank gun position. This is bad news for our armoured carriers. Without fire protection from our guns, it is impossible to advance. Our men are working their way forward by taking advantage of every hollow and furrow. Our *PaK-Wagen* [3.7cm PaK armed SdKfz 251/10] stops: it appears to have been hit; a small cloud of smoke rises as the crew jump out. To avoid any further losses the other vehicles have been positioned behind some adjacent bushes. Some have also been hit, but are still mobile.

Now the Russians lay heavy fire on the PzGren advancing on foot. In the fierce noise of

After the riflemen had dismounted and gone into action, the driver of the halftrack would move the vehicle to a safe position, unless supporting fire from the onboard machine gun was required.

An SdKfz 251 carries a BMW R12 motorcycle. Bush-covered terrain spelt danger for armoured halftracks, since it provided perfect cover for enemy snipers and anti-tank rifle teams.

battle, I hear many clear cries for help. *Gefreiter* Krause, leading the group advancing on our left, is badly hit and has collapsed. My machine gunner No.1 makes a jump forward, but falls backwards to the ground. We cannot help him anymore. The bullet from an anti-tank rifle has completely ripped open the housing on his MG and hit him. Now the other MG of my group is firing one bullet after another into the enemy position. But it is soon recognized by the Russians and comes under fire. We have to recover the MG gunner No.2, who has a badly wounded knee; he is carried to a hollow to receive first aid. Now the Russians, with much loud screaming, attack the rest of our group; two MG gunners and a rifleman attempt to fend them off. Now our SPW are advancing from the right: another counterattack is being driven back. The enemy now concentrates his fire on the vehicles. We are still not making any progress; the Russians are well dug-in and we are outnumbered. Each of our movements is acknowledged with heavy fire. The shells of the mortars howl incessantly and the earth trembles as they explode. The machine gunners on the SPW shoot at the many Russian positions in the forest. *Unteroffizier* Hübner throws hand grenade after hand grenade from his vehicle at the Bolsheviks lying on the ground. But Hübner is too close to the forest, and the Russians are able to throw a grenade into his vehicle. His SPW turns away, and a loud shout for a *Sani* [medic] is heard. The other SPW recognize the danger and turn back. A wild hand-to-hand combat develops and the air is filled with men shouting, bullets whistling and grenades bursting. In the end our armoured carriers have to move back: the enemy is too strong and continues to throw in wave after wave of soldiers.

We should go back too. But how, and who will give us fire cover? Our wounded and dead comrades must be taken with us under all circumstances, and nor must their weapons be left behind.

Suddenly rescue is coming. Our artillery is firing smoke. Laboriously and with great difficulty we work our way back through swamps and reeds, dragging our wounded and dead comrades with us. In the meantime darkness has finally fallen. Our carriers take the wounded with them so that they can quickly be treated. Another takes over the recovery of our fallen comrades and brings them to the cemetery at the rear of our positions.

After contacting II.Btl, we set up night security, since we expect a Russian counterattack, but apart from a number of small patrols, no one has been seen. Perhaps the fighting has done too much damage for them to continue the attack.

Our company has experienced one of its most difficult days. We are proud in the knowledge that we have crushed a Russian battalion. A great success considering the balance of power.

Two SdKfz 251 have been backed into the shallow water at the edge of a lake to allow their crews to thoroughly clean the running gear.

8

1943 – IN COMBAT

During 1942, the *Panzergrenadiere* proved to be an effective support force for the *Panzertruppe* and as a mutual trust grew so did success on the battlefield. The supply of materials and equipment was slowly improving, which allowed the PzGren to undertake even more tasks in addition to their primary duty of supporting the tank forces.

Independent attacks against the flanks of an enemy force
Securing of own flanks and threatened front sections
Extensive combat reconnaissance in and behind enemy lines
Quickly take important sections of terrain

An important prerequisite for the above was for the PzGren to have ability to fight from inside their vehicles and use them only as armoured transport. Unit commanders had recognized that the type had the potential to be developed as the base vehicle for a number of specialized variants. Consequently, military planners began to examine what type of specialist equipment or weapon could be carried (mounted) on a *Schützenpanzerwagen*.

The first improvement was to give the armoured infantry more firepower by installing the 3.7cm PaK on both the light and medium types, which were designated respectively SdKfz 250/10 and SdKfz 251/10. The weapon could fire high-explosive (HE) ammunition which allowed the PzGren to engage effectively in close combat with enemy positions.

The introduction of the SdKfz 250/7 and SdKfz 251/2 – both types mounted the 8cm s GrW 34 – was a considerable improvement, since the crews of this highly effective weapon could now fire at their targets from the interior of the *Panzeraufbau* (armour body).

The SdKfz 251/10 (Ausf A) armed with a 3.7cm PaK were mainly issued to a platoon leader in a PzGren battalion. Although the gun was considered to be obsolete for defeating armour, it was found to be an excellent support weapon when 3.7cm high-explosive ammunition became available in 1940.

The *schwere geländegängiger Protzkraftwagen* (Kfz 69) became the standardized chassis for heavy passenger cars and other vehicles. In a regular (unarmoured) rifle regiment it would be used to tow various guns, including the 15cm s IG 33. This heavy personnel carrier version was designated Kfz 70.

Gun Carriers

In early 1942, the decision to introduce the long-barrelled 7.5cm KwK 40 and StuK 40 for the PzKpfw IV and *Sturmgeschütz*, resulted in a large number of 7.5cm KwK 37 L/24 becoming surplus to requirements. The weapon was first installed in the PzKpfw III Ausf N and also the *schwere Panzerspähwagen Achtrad* (s PzSpWg [8-rad] – heavy armoured car [eight wheeled]). It was then decided to mount the 7.5cm KwK 37 L/24 in the SdKfz 251. Although this was relatively simple to achieve, the large trestle-type mounting for the gun was positioned next to the driver and took up a lot of interior space. After field trials the vehicle was given the designation SdKfz 251/9, and was commonly known to troops on the front as the 'Kanonenwagen'. Since the gun could fire high-explosive (HE) ammunition, the type was considered an ideal addition to the firepower of the armoured infantry. The weapon also fired *Hohlladung* (Hl – shaped or hollow charge) ammunition which was effective against enemy armour.

A new subunit, the *schwere Kanonen-Zug* (heavy gun platoon), was created – detailed in *Kriegstärkenachweisung* (KStN – table of organization) 1125 (gp) dated 21 December 1942 – as part of the heavy company in a PzGrenBtl. It was supplied with one SdKfz 251/1, six 251/9 and one SdKfz 251/4 (IG) as an ammunition carrier. As with all combat vehicles in a heavy company, the *Kanonenwagen* could be assigned to the other companies in the PzGrenBtl according to the situation on the battlefront.

In 1943, the decision was taken to restructure PzGrenKp 'c' (gp), as detailed in KStN 1114 'c' [gp], to improve firepower. A heavy *Zug* (Zg – platoon), equipped with two SdKfz 251/9 and two SdKfz 251/2 armed with the 8cm s GrW34, was assigned to the company.

Some 450 *Kanonenwagen* were produced in 1943, followed by approximately 700 in 1944. The high numbers indicate the importance of the SdKfz 251/9.

Medium Radio Vehicle

At the end of 1942 the decision was taken to produce a new type of radio vehicle based on the SdKfz 251. Although the SdKfz 251/6, *mittlere Kommandopanzerwagen* (m Kdo PzWg – medium armoured command vehicle), was in service as a command/radio vehicle, the troops demanded more specialized variants for various command levels and other purposes. The vehicle was designated SdKfz 251/3, *mittlerer Funkpanzerwagen* (m FuPzWg – medium armoured radio vehicle); confusingly this had been previously issued for the vehicle that towed the 7.5cm le IG 18. The SdKfz 251/4 became the vehicle to tow the gun and transport ammunition.

The most obvious change on the SdKfz 251/3 was the removal of the conspicuous *Rahmenantenne* (frame antenna) which was replaced by a

An SdKfz 251/7 *Pionier-PanzerWagen* (PiPzWg – assault engineer vehicle), has been fitted with a frame antenna taken from an SdKfz 232 *schwerer Panzerspähwagen* (*Achtrad*) (s PzSpWg [8-rad] – heavy armoured car [eight wheeled]). Note a 3kg *Haftholladung* (adhesive hollow charge) has been left on the engine cover.

Sternantenne (star antenna) 'd', with an armoured porcelain insulator which was mounted on the side of the bodywork. The SdKfz 251/3 was available with different combinations of radio equipment:

SdKfz 251/3 I

Equipped with *Funkgerät* (FuG – radio device) 8 and FuG 4 radio, the type was in service with the signal platoons at brigade, regiment and division level.

SdKfz 251/3 II

In addition to FuG 8 and a FuG 4, this variant was also carried a FuG 5. The type was used at battalion level to maintain contact with tank and assault gun units.

SdKfz 251/3 III

This vehicle was equipped with FuG 7 and FuG 1 and was used by a ground-to-air liaison officer to contact officers at division level and also those those in higher echelons.

SdKfz 251/3 IV

Since this variant replaced the SdKfz 251/6, it was consequently fitted with FuG 11 and FuG 12 radio equipment. Many of the original type remained in service until the end of the war.

SdKfz 251/3 V

The vehicle was delivered to reconnaissance battalions and was fitted with a

Kursk 1943: The SdKfz 251/8 *Kranken-Panzerwagen* (armoured ambulance) could be identified, when not marked, by the small fold-down step fitted on the chassis.

FuG 11 radio. If or when required, the *Funksprech* (FuSpr – transceiver) 'f' could also be fitted in an SdKfz 251/3.

Medium Armoured Flamethrower

All German pioneer units would have had flamethrowers in their standard inventory. The first weapons to be introduced on a large scale with the German army, were the portable *Flammenwerfer* (FmW – flamethrower) 35 and FmW 41. The weapon was originally used by the infantry to clear enemy bunkers and other fortifications, but a number of nations began fitting flame equipment to tanks in the years before World War II. Germany had developed their *Flammpanzer* II by 1941, and it was available for use with independent battalion-size units at *Heerestruppen* (army troop) level, but neither the flame-thrower tank nor the distribution proved effective. In 1943, a new version, the *Flammpanzer* III, was delivered to the Panzer regiment staff company, but again the type was also of limited value.

In January 1943 a new approach was taken: it was decided to develop a flamethrower variant of the SdKfz 251. It was to have two flame projectors, each with 14mm nozzles and fitted with armoured shields, mounted – inside the vehicle – on brackets attached to the side walls. A third portable flame

An SdKfz 251/1 follows a tank attack. The 7.92mm *Maschinengewehr* (MG – machine gun) 42 is not mounted but has the integral bipod folded down. Note the PzKpfw III *Beobachtungswagen* (PzBeobWg – armoured observation vehicle) in the background.

Two SdKfz 251/6 *Kommando-Panzerwagen* (KdoPzWg – armoured command vehicle) of *Panzernachrichten-Abteilung* (PzNachrAbt – armoured signals battalion) 128 attached to 23.PzDiv, which was part of Heeresgruppe Süd (Army Group South) in southern Russia. The camouflage pattern was applied by the unit to match the terrain of the battlefront.

projector, with 7mm nozzle, was carried on the outside of the rear door. A pump for the flame propellant was powered by a two-stroke engine mounted at the rear of the crew compartment. (This meant that the rear doors could not be used.) The flame propellant was stored in two 350-litre tanks. Flamethrower equipment was originally mounted on SdKfz 251 Ausf C and SdKfz 251 Ausf D, but the portable flamethrower was dropped as production continued. The type was designated SdKfz 251/16.

In service they were organized, according to KStN 1130, into *Teileinheit* (TE – subunit) *Flammzug* (flame platoon) or *Flammenwerfer-Zug* (flame-weapon platoon), each supplied with six vehicles. This platoon was attached to the newly introduced *Stabskompanie* (headquarters company) in a PzGrenRgt (gp).

In June 1943, PzGrenRgt 103 (14.PzDiv) distributed a leaflet explaining the intended use of the *mittlerer Flammpanzerwagen* (m Fl PzWg – medium armoured flame-thrower vehicle):

The m Fl PzWg is intended to fight pockets of enemy resistance, armoured cars and bunkers and will also be used during house-to-house fighting. The flamethrower vehicle can be deployed at a range of up to 40m, against enemy personnel, flammable and hard targets. The *Maschinengewehr* (MG – machine gun) 34 is used against troops at maximum range of 400m.

The m Fl PzWg will be used in most cases within the *Flamm-Zug*, but always in close cooperation with mounted PzGren (gp) units.

The *Flamm-Panzerwagen* cannot be used on the frontline as an escort tank or assault gun, nor must it be used as the leading vehicle for combat or during a march. Finally, it is strictly forbidden for the type to be deployed for security tasks or as an independent reconnaissance squad. Such use will inevitably lead to the early loss of this effective weapon. When fighting under special conditions – against field bunkers, permanent fortifications or against strongpoints in the battle for a village – an individual m Fl PzWg can be attached to other mounted PzGren (gp) fighting units.

When the crew dismount to fight on foot, the m Fl PzWg are to be left or sent back with the armoured carriers of the platoon. The *Flamm-Zug* can be deployed to support a counterattack, but this must involve all available m Fl PzWg.

During the attack the m Fl PzWg proceed in line behind the mounted PzGren. The flamethrowers may only be used on specific orders in dense mist.

Three *mittlerer geländegäniger Lastkraftwagen* (m gel Lkw – medium cross-country vehicles) of our supply squadron each carry two drums of flame propellant: a total of 8,400 litres.

Two SdKfz 251/6, in service with 23.PzDiv, ready to be transported to Heeresgruppe Süd for operations in the Caucasus. The nearest carrier has been fitted with two *Fahrzeug-Antennenfuss* (vehicle aerial mount), while the other has the standard-type antenna for armoured vehicles.

An SdKfz 251/1 in service with the *Aufklärungs-Abteilung* (AufklAbt – reconnaissance battalion) of PzGrenDiv *Grossdeutschland*: note the white *Stahlhelm* (steel helmet) symbol. The camouflage scheme is one of a number used on vehicles operating in southern Russia.

Left: The commanding officer, *Oberst* Smilo Freiherr von Lüttwitz and his staff officers, take the salute at the parade to mark the formation of 26.PzDiv on 14 September 1942. The SdKfz 251/10 (Ausf C) carries the name 'Friedericus Rex' and also the emblem, a sword on a white shield, of I./PzGrenRgt 9.

Below: The SdKfz 10/5 offered little protection for the crew, especially in foul weather. The wire cage was positioned to catch shell cases as the gun fired.

Above: In September 1941, the Steyr 1500 began to replace the Horch as the standard heavy cross-country car. The vehicle was powered by a 3,500cc Steyr V8 air-cooled petrol engine, all-wheel drive and simple, but rugged, conventional leaf spring suspension. Some 12,450 chassis had been completed by March 1944.

Right: An original table: A typical PzGrenRgt issued with an armoured carrier battalion.

On 10 July 1943, the staff company of PzGrenRgt 9 submitted an after-action report on the deployment of the *Flamm-Zug* (FlZg – flame-thrower platoon):

Flamethrower

a. The two-stage centrifugal pump delivers a maximum pressure of 15 atmospheres [220psi], as a consequence we achieved flame ranges of only 35m to 40m.

It is absolutely important to turn the release trigger firmly upwards in order to completely shut the valve.

b. If the valve is not closed completely, a jet of propellant is deflected sideways due the muzzle cap being closed. Depending on the position of the pipe, the burning propellant splashes along the side or into the interior of the vehicle.

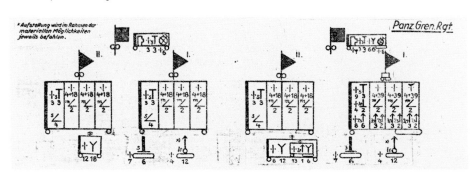

1943: armoured personnel carrier company.

Panzergrenadier-Kompanie c (gp) (KStN 1114c)
PzGrenRgt 114, 6.PzDiv, structure as of 1 April 1943

Grp Führer*	1. Zug	2. Zug	3. Zug	4. (schwerer) Zug	Kfz Inst-Zug	Gefechts-Tross**	Gepäck-Tross
SdKfz 251/3	SdKfz 251/10 3,7 cm	SdKfz 251/10 3,7 cm	SdKfz 251/10 3,7 cm	(motorcycle)	Lkw 3 t	le gl Pkw	Lkw 3 t
SdKfz 251/3	SdKfz 251/1	SdKfz 251/1	SdKfz 251/1	SdKfz 251/3	SdKfz 10	SdKfz 3	
(motorcycle)	SdKfz 251/1	SdKfz 251/1	SdKfz 251/1	SdKfz 251/2 8 cm	SdKfz 3	SdKfz 3	
(motorcycle)	SdKfz 251/1	SdKfz 251/1	SdKfz 251/1	SdKfz 251/2 8 cm	SdKfz 7	SdKfz 3	
(motorcycle)				SdKfz 251/9 7,5 cm		SdKfz 3	
(motorcycle)				SdKfz 251/9 7,5 cm		SdKfz 3	
						SdKfz 3	
						SdKfz 3	

* Provision with SdKfz 2 *Kettenkrad* for deployment in the east.

** Optional provision with SdKfz 3 *Maultier* for high cross-country mobility, replacement by standard 3t truck possible.

The heavy company introduced the SdKfz 251/9 *Kanonenwagen*.

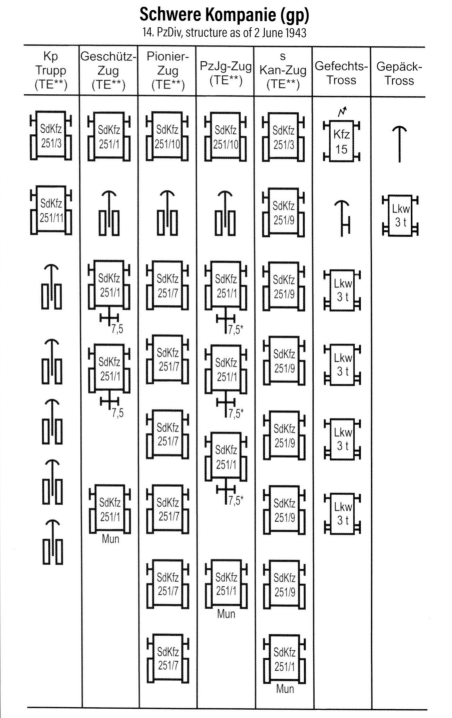

	Schwere Kompanie (gp) 14. PzDiv, structure as of 2 June 1943					
Kp Trupp (TE)**	**Geschütz-Zug (TE**)**	**Pionier-Zug (TE**)**	**PzJg-Zug (TE**)**	**s Kan-Zug (TE**)**	**Gefechts-Tross**	**Gepäck-Tross**
SdKfz 251/3	SdKfz 251/1	SdKfz 251/10	SdKfz 251/10	SdKfz 251/3	Kfz 15	↑
SdKfz 251/11				SdKfz 251/9		Lkw 3 t
	SdKfz 251/1 7,5	SdKfz 251/7	SdKfz 251/1 7,5*	SdKfz 251/9	Lkw 3 t	
	SdKfz 251/1 7,5	SdKfz 251/7	SdKfz 251/1 7,5*	SdKfz 251/9	Lkw 3 t	
		SdKfz 251/7	SdKfz 251/1 7,5*	SdKfz 251/9	Lkw 3 t	
	SdKfz 251/1 Mun	SdKfz 251/7		SdKfz 251/9	Lkw 3 t	
		SdKfz 251/7	SdKfz 251/1 Mun	SdKfz 251/9		
		SdKfz 251/7		SdKfz 251/1 Mun		

* 7.5cm PaK 40 or 7.62cm PaK (r).

** TE (*Teileinheiten*) were standardized subunits with dedicated KStN.

c. The pilot flame continues to burn for some 60 seconds even after the Bowden cable is released. This means that the muzzle does not cool down and the propellant jet remains hot, making it more difficult to fight effectively against bunkers and houses.

e. A considerable part of the flame propellant does not burn or burns imperfectly. It must be examined whether 100 percent combustion could be achieved by changing the composition of the propellant.

Equipment

a. Better eye and face protection is required against the flame chemicals; propellant splashes cannot be avoided, especially in windy conditions. The corrosive effect causes skin damage, as timely removal will not always be possible.

b. The connecting wires for the throat-type microphone and also the headphones [FuSpr 'f'] are too short; the flame operator has no freedom of movement to fire the onboard machine gun.

c. Replace the carrying brackets for rifles, with brackets for the machine guns. Each of the three trucks must have two loading spars for unloading the drums of propellant.

Organization

A *Flammzug-Führer* [platoon commander] cannot command the platoon from his *Flamm-Panzerwagen* if they are 500m apart in combat. Therefore, a *Flamm-Führer* must be appointed for the platoon leader vehicle.

Both the SdKfz 10/4 and SdKfz 10/5 were always deployed close to the battlefront and inevitably losses began to mount. In an attempt to improve survivability a set of armour plates was produced, primarily to protect the driver and co-driver, and which would be fitted in field workshops.

Production

With the reappointment of Heinz Guderian – he had been removed from his post after the failure to capture Moscow in 1941 – as *Generalinspekteurs der Panzertruppe* (Inspector General of the Armoured Corps) in February 1943, the listing of production data was revised.

For reasons unknown, the statistics for armament production and delivery

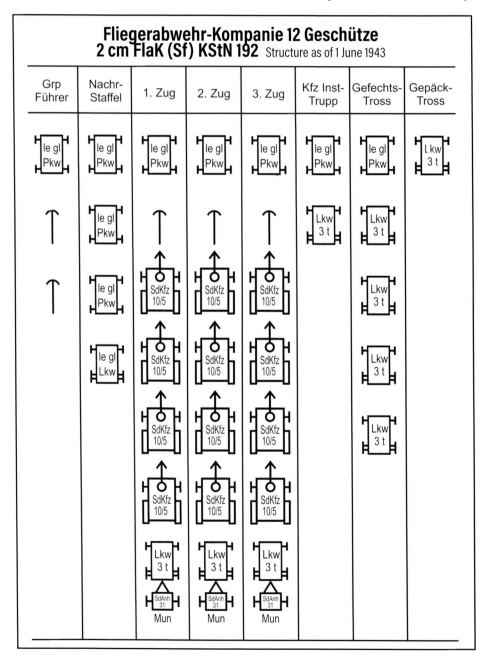

Fliegerabwehr-Kompanie 12 Geschütze							
2 cm FlaK (Sf) KStN 192 Structure as of 1 June 1943							
Grp Führer	Nachr-Staffel	1. Zug	2. Zug	3. Zug	Kfz Inst-Trupp	Gefechts-Tross	Gepäck-Tross

The SturmFlaK-Kp (Sf) had 12 guns.

between December 1942 and April 1943 are not in German archives, but more precise listings do begin again in May 1943 and list the current stocks of selected variants.

It is interesting that in the case of the light armoured carrier only two variants were listed individually, the SdKfz 250/10 (with 3.7cm PaK) and the SdKfz 250/9 (with a turret-mounted 2cm KwK 38 L/55). All other variants,

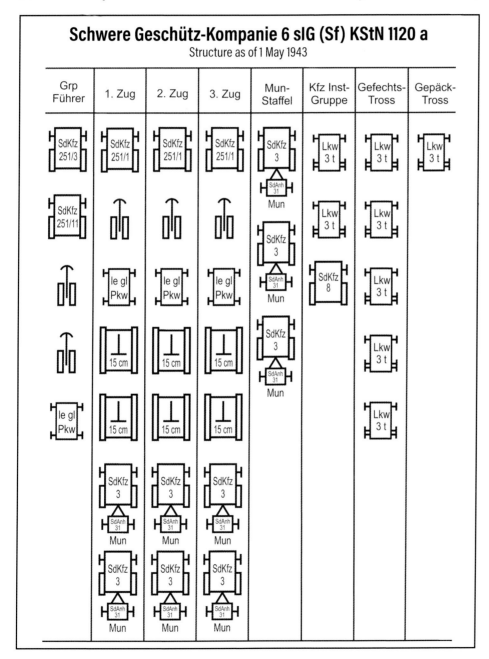

Schwere Geschütz-Kompanie 6 sIG (Sf) KStN 1120 a

Structure as of 1 May 1943

From 1943, each PzGrenRgt had a self-propelled artillery company issued with 15cm *schwere Infanteriegeschütz auf Geschützwagen* 38(t) (s IG 33 auf Gw 38(t) – heavy infantry gun on PzKpfw 38[t] chassis). The type was designated SdKfz 138/1 and was known as the *Grille* (cricket).

Clearly marked with Red Cross insignia, an SdKfz 251/7 *Kranken-Panzerwagen* (armoured ambulance) is being prepared for duty. Note that the antenna for the radio is mounted on the armoured roof plate, directly above the radio operator.

including the most important one in terms of numbers, the SdKfz 250/1, were again counted together.

The situation was similar for the medium armoured carrier. Here again the SdKfz 251/10 armed with the 3.7cm PaK and the *Kanonenwagen*, the variant armed with the 7.5cm cannon were counted. The stocks of the remaining variants including the SdKfz 251/1 were listed together.

It is difficult to find a reason for this approach. On the one hand, the *Waffenamt* (ordnance office) seemed to fundamentally underestimate the relevance of the basic versions when maintaining the lists.

PzDiv 43

Immediately after his reinstatement in 1943, *Generaloberst* Heinz Guderian began to plan a number of fundamental changes to the organizational structure of the Panzer division. The introduction PzKpfw V Panther into service in mid-1943, suddenly (and effectively) improved the combat capability of the *Panzerwaffe* (armoured forces). Initially the plan was to equip one of the two Panzer battalions in a Panzer division with four companies, each with 17 PzKpfw V Panther. The number of tanks would eventually be increased to 22.

1943	le SPW production	250/10 stock	250/9 stock	other stock
January	127		*	
February	288		*	
March	289	101	32	1,652
April	210	115	32	1,808
May	250	112	46	1,850
June	271	123	93	2,066
July	251	127	128	2,311
August	290	**	**	**
September	279	132	222	2,316
October	252	127	256	2,317
November	73	124	303	2,406
December	318	118	301	2,498

1943	m SPW production	251/10 stock	251/9 stock	other stock
January	126		3,427	
February	125		3,206	
March	150	96	95	1,250
April	230	89	115	1,305
May	251	100	139	1,354
June	259	136	139	1,507
July	303	147	163	1,765
August	432	**	**	**
September	627	127	156	2,293
October	526	130	202	2,684
November	657	138	245	3,086
December	572	123	298	3,442

* numbers combined with m SPW   ** not available

An SdKfz 251/1 (Ausf C) towing a 15cm sIG 33 has fallen victim to the *Rasputitsa* (mud season) in Russia. The vehicle has received a coating of whitewash camouflage and is in service with 5.SS-PzDiv Wiking. Note the crew has named their vehicle 'Nürnberg'.

After the D-Day landings on 6 June 1944, military movements in France during daylight hours could be hazardous, since Allied ground-attack aircraft roamed the sky unchallenged searching for targets. All vehicles, like this SdKfz 251/9 *Kanonenwagen* would be camouflaged with foliage, and moved rapidly from cover to cover.

Above: An SdKfz 251/1 from 3.PzDiv races through a Russian village on the Kursk salient during *Unternehmen Zitadelle* (Operation *Citadel*) which was launched on 5 July 1943. Interestingly, those units that were issued with armoured personnel carriers suffered significantly fewer battle casualties.

Right: A SdKfz 251/10 of PzRgt Hermann Göring, a *Luftwaffe* field unit. The regiment was positioned on Sicily when Allied forces began landing (Operation *Husky*) on 9 July 1943, and fought until it was withdrawn to the Italian mainland.

Instead of *motorisiert* (motorized) towed PaK and self-propelled types, the divisional *Panzer-Jäger-Abteilung* (PzJgAbt – anti-tank battalion) was to be fully equipped with *Sturmgeschütz* (four companies each with 22 StuG). Furthermore, first drafts of PzDiv 43 structure showed PzKpfw VI Tiger Ausf E-equipped battalions attached to the division for combat at focal points.

If these ambitious goals had been achieved, the Panzer divisions, without doubt, would have been significantly strengthened and the effectiveness of the

Wehrmacht considerably improved. However, the parlous state of the German armaments industry doomed the plan to be nothing more than hypothetical.

The artillery regiment in each Panzer division was significantly strengthened with a *Panzer-Artillerie-Abteilung* (PzArtAbt – armoured artillery battalion) equipped with 18 self-propelled howitzers.

What had been the *Kradschützen* battalion now became *Panzer-Aufklärungs-Abteilung* (armoured reconnaissance battalion), which was well equipped with SdKfz 250 armoured halftracks, *Panzerspähwagen* (armoured reconnaissance vehicles) and also *schwere Kompanie* (gp) (heavy armoured companies); in terms of combat capability it was very similar to that of a PzGrenBtl (gp).

Improvements were also planned at all levels of the PzGren. The two PzGenRgt (each with two battalions) were to be directly attached to the command staff of the Panzer division and, as a consequence, the brigade staff of the PzGrenRgt was disbanded.

One battalion (of two) in each PzGrenRgt was to be armoured and fully equipped with *Schützenpanzerwagen*. But this requirement could not be implemented, and only one of the four battalion in the division was issued with a full complement of armoured personnel carriers.

However, two important demands were to be implemented. Each PzGrenRgt received a self-propelled heavy infantry gun company (six 15cm sIG 33 on PzKpfw 38(t) *Grille* [cricket]) and a SturmFlaK company with 12 SdKfz 10/5 (armed with 2cm FlaK 38).

The white *Stahlhelm* (steel helmet) emblem of PzGrenDiv Grossdeutschland is prominent on this SdKfz 251/1 *Schützenpanzerwagen* (SchtzPzWg – armoured personnel carrier). In July 1943, the division was attached to Heeresgruppe Süd (Army Group South) in the Caucasus and then on the Kursk salient.

Above: Elements of an armoured division advance across the Steppe landscape typical of the Kursk salient. The force includes SdKfz 251 medium halftracks, PzKpfw III and 2cm Sturmflak.

Right: This SdKfz 251/3 *Funkpanzerwagen* (armoured radio vehicle) is in service with the divisional signal battalion of PzGrenDiv Grossdeutschland. The vehicle is painted in southern Russia-style camouflage.

Left: The SdKfz 251/9 *Kanonenwagen* quickly became the most effective weapon in the inventory of both the PzGrenKp 'c' (gp) and s Kp (gp).

Below: The crew of this SdKfz 10/5 in service with a *Luftwaffe* unit has attempted to conceal their vehicle under piled-up snow. Note the *Schwebekreisvisier* (pendulum ring sight) 38 mounted on the gun.

The SdKfz 251/10 to the right has been fitted with 'unofficial' additional armour, whereas the crew of the other vehicle has used spare track links. Both were officially prohibited.

These reorganizations, which became effective in autumn 1943, were intended not only to increase the fighting power but also to reduce the number of battlefield casualties and equipment losses.

The combat strength of the PzGrenBt (gp) could be considerably increased when compared to an unarmoured battalion.

After the end of the Kursk campaign, Kamfgruppe Zimmermann of 20.PzDiv submitted an after-action report on 28 July 1943. The unit consisted of I./PzGrenRgt 10 and a *Panzerkompanie* commanded by *Leutnant* Bussmann, was deployed at Peshkova northeast of Oryol:

Authorized weaponry PzGrenKp and s Kp within PzGrenBtl

	MG 34	s MG 34	8cm m GrW	12cm s GrW	3.7cm PaK	7.5cm s PaK	7.5cm le IG	SdKfz 251/9
Tactical symbols *								
SchtzKp 1940 (3.PzDiv)	18	Four	Two (5cmGrW)	-	-	-	-	-
PzGrenKp (mot) PzDiv 43	18	Four	Two	-	-	-	-	-
PzGrenKp (gp) PzDiv 43	39	Four	Two	-	Three	-	Six	Two
s Kp + MG Kp 1940	Four	Eight	Six	-	Three	-	Two	-
s Kompanie (mot) PzDiv 43	Three	-	-	Four	-	Three	-	-
s Kompanie (gp) PzDiv 43	21	-	-	-	-	Three	Two	Six

At 02:00hrs, the commander received orders at the regiment command post to come to readiness on the Vetrovo-Zemyanski line and prepare to repel an enemy attack at Point 233.0. At 03:00hrs the tanks took up a concealed position on the rear slope west of Point 222.4. The SPW was standing by in a hollow to the south.

Some 22 enemy tanks were detected at Point 233.0. In order to challenge them to attack, our right wing was withdrawn as conspicuously as possible. This deceptive move was successful and the enemy attacked. A short and fierce firefight followed, in which 24 enemy tanks were destroyed; three were US types. We had no losses.

At 09:00hrs a very effective attack by StuKa dive bombers took place on enemy positions, during which eight tanks and an assault gun became stuck in a marshy depression. Taking advantage of the situation, our battle group initiated a counterattack. Despite heavy defensive fire from enemy troops in well-camouflaged positions, our attack quickly gained ground. The PzGren of 20.PzDiv, following the attack, dismounted and began mopping up pockets of enemy resistance on the battlefield. At 12:00hrs, riflemen of 2.Kp, reinforced by a company of tanks, reached Point 233.0. The second tank company was positioned to protect the right flank as the PzGren regained their old positions.

The PzGren on the left came under heavy flanking fire from enemy positioned northwest of Vetrovo. Consequently, three SPW and a *Kanonenwagen* were deployed to take these positions. While the *Kanonenwagen* covered the position with continuous fire, the armoured carriers quickly started to attack with their crews firing all on-board weapons and throwing hand grenades. Enemy infantry were driven out of their fox holes; some

Increasing demand for the SdKfz 251, meant that the bodywork had to be fabricated using rivets and not welding. In 1942, only one company, Bohemia based in Ceska Lipa, was involved.

Above: Although both types of armoured halftracks had excellent off-road performance, their *Schachtellaufwerk* (interleaved running gear) easily became clogged by deep mud or frozen snow. This vehicle is an SdKfz 251/1 Ausf C with riveted bodywork.

Right: The emblem, a ski in a white ring, stencilled on the rear on the rear of this SdKfz 10/5, identifies it as being in service with 1.Ski-Jäger Division.

were captured but many were killed. Once again, the PzGren were able to re-occupy their old positions.

At 13:00hrs the commander reported the execution of the order, and at 15:00hrs the combat group was relieved by PzAbt 21.

The enemy did not initiate any counterattacks having suffered severe losses in men and equipment. The *Kampfgruppe* [battle group] achieved an outstanding success on this day by destroying 30 enemy tanks, including six US-built heavies, without any losses. In addition, PzAbt 21 destroyed another 15 tanks and an assault gun. Those enemy tanks that were bogged down and abandoned were blown up by our troops. More than 130 prisoners were taken and a large number of weapons and equipment captured. We estimate the enemy lost some 300 men.

The s IG (Sfl) *Kompanie*

The 15cm *schwere Infanteriegeschütz* (s IG – heavy infantry gun) 33 was integral equipment in all rifle units. The weapon, which was towed by an SdKfz 10 or SdKfz 11, soon became an important support gun in a rifle regiment.

The clearance of obstacles was a regular task for the men of the *Panzerpioniere* (armoured engineers). An SdKfz 251/7 *Pionier-Panzerwagen* (PiPzWg – armoured engineer carrier) Ausf C here carries two 8,000kg-capacity *Übergangsschienen* (bridging sections).

In 1940, a number of tank divisions had been assigned a company of six 15cm s IG 33 on PzKpfw I (Ausf B), *Selbstfahrlafette* (Sfl – self-propelled). Despite various problems with the totally overloaded and mechanically unreliable chassis, the vehicles had shown great potential. Military planners immediately began the search for a more suitable chassis on which to mount the weapon, but they were thwarted due to the production situation in the German armaments industry.

It was 1943 before a new self-propelled gun carriage was produced by using the chassis of the Czech-built PzKpfw 38(t) Ausf H. Little by little, the Panzer divisions received two companies, one for each PzGrenRgt.

In October 1942, the 26.PzDiv was based in Amiens, France, in the same area as 15.Armee, and equipped with French-built (or captured) equipment. The division was ordered to prepare for transfer to Italy, while at the same time converting to German-built tanks. 26.PzDiv was only partially operational when it arrived in Italy, during July 1943, but nevertheless, both battalions in one of its elements, 67.PzGrenRgt, had each been equipped with a company of six 15cm sIG 33 (Sfl).

In July 1943 the unit had already begun to complain about the lack of SdKfz 251/3 for the staff section of each s IG (Sfl) company. The *Maultier* (mule) half-track trucks assigned for transporting ammunition were also

Above: The crew of this SdKfz 251/9, mounting a 7.5cm *Sturmkanone* (StuK – assault gun) 37 L/24, have camouflaged their vehicle by concealing it under sheaves of straw.

Far left: A self-propelled 15cm sIG 33 auf Gw 38(t) Ausf H built on the unchanged hull of the PzKpfw 38(t); the later Ausf M had a front mounted engine. Both types were known to troops in the field as the *Grille* (cricket) and their mobility as support weapons was much appreciated by the PzGren.

The SdKfz 10/4 mounting the earlier 2cm FlaK 30, is recognizable by the shape of the gun shield and that of the muzzle brake. The vehicle has been fitted with an armour kit by a field workshop.

criticized: the vehicle had been designed for deployment on the *Ost* (East) Front, and seemed unsuited to the drier conditions on the Italian battlefront. A more obvious reason the unit demanded armoured ammunitions carriers was that the *Maultier* was soft-skinned, which severely restricted deployment.

On 17 October 1943, 67.PzGrenRgt submitted an after-action report:

1.) Equipment

The s IG (Sfl) has essentially proved its worth during operations in Italy. The advantages over the s IG being towed by trucks are obvious. The armoured and manoeuvrable Sfl is well suited for rapid deployment on the battlefront. When driving on mountain roads, the Sfl 38(t) was responsive even when negotiating sharp curves. The engine is sufficiently powerful, and the only difficulties occur in wet weather, which causes thick mud. In October, it was virtually impossible to leave the solid ground to take up a firing position. In these cases, it was always necessary to position the Sfl on a paved road. But we often had a problem with the reverse gear as the gun was manoeuvred into position.

2.) Suggestions for improvements

The space of the gunner to operate the gun laying mechanism is too narrow. The radio, which is operated by the loader, is almost impossible to use during a battle: the most suitable place would be adjacent to the commander. In this were done, the three rounds of ammunition stored on the left of the gunner could be relocated to the loader's space. Furthermore, the front of the gun mounting must be fitted with a cover to prevent rainwater from dripping on the driver during bad weather. The lack of spare parts caused 9.Kp considerable difficulties; not one of our spare parts depots in Italy could supply snap rings for track pins. Our operational readiness is seriously compromised.

3.) Organization

The sIG 33/1 (Sfl) is designed as an offensive weapon, but 9.Kp was not able to gain any experience in this respect, since the vehicle was only used for two attacks during the deployment in Italy. In the battles during the retreat operations the *gepanzerte Selbstfahrlafette* [gep Sfl – armoured self-propelled] gun has proved its worth when deployed close to the frontline. To date we have not suffered any total losses, despite the enemy artillery being very accurate.

4.) Equipment

As already described in the last experience report, the tactical operation suffered from a lack of signals equipment which complicated the deployment of the entire s IG company. The lack of radio equipment was pointed out several times. However, the subsequent allocation of a 30W transmitter in the SPW only remedied one deficiency. At least the company is now able to maintain a secure radio contact with the battalion.

When the more powerful 2cm FlaK 38 became available for mounting on the light halftrack, the designation was changed to SdKfz 10/5. The vehicle has been fitted with extra armour.

The SdKFz 251/6 (Ausf C) *Kommando-Panzerwagen* (KdoPzWg – armoured command vehicle) was used by senior commanders and signal units. A significant number of this variant survived until end of the war.

5.) General remarks

The s IG 33/1 auf Sfl is not suited to the light sandy soil encountered in Italy. In general, very poor road conditions always meant that a commander had to seek out hard-surfaced roads. This would not be the case if the gun was attached to an SdKfz 11 tractor.

The after-action report is interesting. Italy is divided north-to-south by the Apennine mountains and is crossed by many steeply inclined roads and tracks, each having numerous tight bends. During the battle for the country, many German armoured units were decimated by mechanical failures as they crossed from east to west. Many experience reports written at the time illustrate the inadequacy of all German tanks: their final drives and steering gear were not sufficiently robust to handle the long, steep climbs and hairpin bends. But the PzKpfw 38(t) chassis was one of the few that could cope with these conditions.

12cm *Granatwerfer*

At the beginning of *Unternehmen* Barbarossa, German units were issued with two different types of *Granatwerfer* (GrW – grenade launcher [mortar]); the

5cm *leichter Granatwerfer* (le GrW – light grenade launcher [mortar]) 36 and the 8cm *schwerer Granatwerfer* (s GrW – heavy grenade launcher [mortar]) 34.

However, the Red Army was equipped with the much heavier 12cm mortar (120mm Polkovoi Minomjot obr 193) which had a superior range and explosive effect and gave their infantry a valuable advantage in trench warfare. As the advance into Russia continued, German troops were ordered to collect any captured or abandoned mortars and return them to a holding depot. In 1942, these captured weapons began to be issued to German units as 12cm GrW 378(r).

The performance of the weapon was exceptional and this convinced officials in the *Waffenamt* that it must be replicated by a German manufacturer. The weapon was designated as the 12cm *schwerer Granatwerfer* (GrW – grenade launcher [mortar]) 42.

A comparison of ballistic performance shows that the 12cm s GrW 42 significantly exceeded that of the 8cm s GrW 34 and even the 15cm s IG 33 infantry gun. There was also a practical advantage, in that it was sufficiently lightweight to be moved by a light motor vehicle.

In December 1942, 26.InfDiv was ordered to carry out a troop trial, but the results are not known. Production began in January 1943 and 76 units had been delivered by the end of the month. Military planners decided that

An SdKfz 251/16 *Flamm-Panzerwagen* (armoured flame thrower), military planners authorized six of the type to be issued to each PzRgt or PzPiBtl. Note the propellant hose for a portable *Flammenwerfer* mounted across the rear doors.

the weapon was initially to be delivered only to independent grenade launcher [mortar] battalions at army group level, since the mortar was easier to move than a heavy infantry gun. Their decision is not surprising given the production problems of German tractors.

	5cm le GrW 36	8cm s GrW 34	12cm s GrW 42	15cm s IG 33
Shell size	5cm	8cm	12cm	15cm
Range (maximum)	520m	1,900m	6,000m	4,650m
Shell weight	0.915kg	3.5kg	15.8kg	38kg
Muzzle velocity	75mps	152mps	283mps	240mps
Number of charges	One	Four	Six	Six
Rate of fire per min	30	30	8–10	1–2
Weight (ready to fire)	14kg	56.7kg	285kg	1,750kg
Weight (travelling)	14kg	56.7kg	560kg	1,750kg

The SdKfz 251/1 carried three 7.92mm *Maschinengewehr* (MG – machine gun) 34, of which two were mounted, as on this vehicle. The rear machine gun could be used for anti-aircraft defence and is fitted with a *Patronentrommel* (saddle-drum magazine).

Apparently the PzGren in the Panzer divisions began to receive small numbers of 12cm s GrW 42 in the summer 1943, but how they were allocated is not known. Some PzGrenKp were issued with one or two s GrW 42 instead of the s GrW 34, whereas three or four s GrW 42 were supplied only to the heavy companies of a PzGrenBtl.

PzGrenDiv

In mid-1943, the decision was taken to reorganize all available motorized infantry divisions as PzGren divisions. Despite the name these units remained under the authority and responsibility of the infantry.

The PzGrenDiv was issued with a PzAbt, which despite the name was normally equipped with *Sturmgeschütze* rather than tanks. The infantry elements were named grenadier, in contrast to PzGren in the Panzer divisions. The organization of the Grenadier Regiment (GrenRgt) was almost the same as that of the 1940-type *Schützenregiment*. Armoured personnel carriers were not issued to the grenadier companies on a regular basis. Only the reconnaissance battalion would be supplied with armoured carriers.

Because of a general shortage of armoured personnel carriers, PzGren divisions could not adopt the proven tactical methods employed by the Panzer divisions, since they could not follow the assault guns as a closed formation.

Two sections of *Brückengerät* (bridging equipment) 'K' have been positioned over a water obstacle. Building bridges during the *Rasputitsa* in Russia could be difficult. The area is being protected by an SdKfz 10/4 (2cm FlaK 30): Note the vehicle has the letter 'K' for Armeegruppe (Army Group) Kleist and the marking for 6.PzDiv.

Above: An SdKfz 251/9 (Ausf D) on display at an open day held, on 19 March 1944, at the *Ersatz und Ausbildungs Brigade* (mixed training brigade) of PzGrenDiv Grossdeutschland in Cottbus. Note the propaganda poster portraying an enemy agent.

Right: The SdKfz 10/5 gave the crew little protection from enemy fire and the weather; the freezing cold and constantly being wet were probably their most dangerous enemy.

Above: The gunner has lowered the 2cm FlaK 30 to its maximum depression to engage enemy positions in a valley.

Right: An SdKfz 10/5 mounting a 2cm FlaK 38 fitted with a *Schwebekreisvisier* (pendulum ring sight) for the gunner.

9

1944 – DEFENDING THE REICH

While the *Panzergrenadiere* had been able to demonstrate their capabilities on many battlefronts during 1943, the decisive battle was to be lost. *Unternehmen Zitadelle* (Operation *Citadel*), the major operation on the Kursk salient planned for the summer, was intended not only to straighten the front and destroy large parts of the Red Army, but to create the conditions for the build-up of German operational reserves. This operation failed.

German tank wedges were able to penetrate Soviet positions, especially in the southern part. Had it been possible to use the strategic advantage, the tanks could have attacked and destroyed the Russian reserves in the rear. However, despite all German tactical principles, the Panzers performed as almost isolated units. Neither the German infantry divisions nor the poorly equipped PzGren units were able to follow local breakthroughs. Thus, the attack at Kursk failed partly because of lacking sufficient PzGren units, which would have been able to defeat the enemy anti-tank defences and dug-in machine-gun and also artillery positions.

When the western Allies landed on Sicily, the German army had finally lost the game for strategic initiative.

Bagration

On 23 June 1944, the great summer offensive, *Operatsiya* (Operation) Bagration, planned by the *Stavka Glavnogo Komandovaniya* (Stavka – main command of the armed forces) was launched by the Red Army against Heeresgruppe Mitte (Army Group Centre): by 28 June, 4.Armee had been destroyed, while both 3.Panzerarmee and 9.Armee were virtually annihilated. These massive attacks led to the total loss of 25 divisions and, despite the arrival of more armoured units, a catastrophe could not be prevented. The battlefront featured areas of

German field engineers have cut out a section of the superstructure on a battle-damaged Soviet T-34 for a PzGren machine gun team, armed with a *Maschinengewehr* (MG – machine gun) 42, to establish a firing position.

The SdKfz 251/17 was armed with a 2cm FlaK gun as a *Selbstfahrlafette* (Sfl – self-propelled) anti-aircraft vehicle. The type was highly valued by the PzGren, since it could be used effectively against ground targets and soft-skinned or light armoured vehicles.

dense woodland, here the PzGren battalions were indispensable for supporting any deployment by the few available tanks. The dogged defence put up by the Panzer divisions (supported by PzGren) and *Sturmgeschütz* battalions allowed German forces to hold important sections, including that between the Berezina and Njemen rivers, as the Red Army offensive ran out of impetus.

A similar situation occurred a month later when Heeresgruppe Nordukraine (Army Group North Ukraine) was facing annihilation, but it was saved by a number of counterattacks by 1.PzDiv, 8.PzDiv and 24.PzDiv. Their actions not only prevented a catastrophe but also made it possible for a frontline to be established along the San and Vistula rivers.

20.PzDiv

In mid-1943, 20.PzDiv was attached to Heeresgruppe Mitte and heavily involved in the battles on the Kursk salient. At the beginning of 1944, the unit was being reorganized to allow one of its four PzGrenBtl to be equipped with armoured personnel carriers. The work took place in the field: the drivers of the carriers had to be trained and the riflemen had to learn new tactics.

On 1 March 1944, the division reported that 42 out of an authorized 93 PzKpfw IV as operational and the number of light and medium armoured infantry carriers, armoured cars and artillery observers' vehicles amounted to 127 of the 271 authorized.

On 8 March, 20.PzDiv submitted an after-action report, which dealt with the defensive battles of the last few months, at which point only a limited number of SdKfz 251 were available:

General issues:

It is the task of a Panzer division to stand by as a reserve to attack focal points with a combination of speed and firepower. In the last few months, our division could only be deployed in such a way in rare instances. The danger of our subunits being attacked and dispersed must be taken particularly seriously in any heavy defensive battle, but this could not always be avoided. Therefore, the division must never be deployed as a combined reserve. Often the tanks, since the formation of the armoured personnel carrier battalion, and other infantry fighting vehicles have been redistributed to several divisions on orders from high command.

Combat by PzGren

Attack operations have shown repeatedly that they succeed provided there has been sufficient time allowed for thorough a reconnaissance. An unplanned attack against an

The VW Typ 166 *Schwimmwagen* (swimming vehicle) was a versatile vehicle; not only did it float, but it also had excellent cross-country mobility. The type was built by VW at their facilities in Wolfsburg and also by Porsche in Stuttgart; the body (hull) was produced by Ambi Budd Presswerke of Berlin.

Above: A desperate shortage of equipment caused front-line engineer units to use whatever was available, including *Luftwaffe* items. Here an SdKfz 251/1 has been fitted with a 20mm MG 151/20 *Kraftgesteuerter Drehturm* (powered turret) mounting as used in a Junkers Ju 188 medium bomber.

Right: A *Flammschütze* (flame-thrower operator) of a SdKfz 251/16 *Flammpanzerwagen* (armoured flame-thrower vehicle).

enemy defensive position should never be ordered, since success is unlikely and our losses will be high. The attack should, preferably, be timed for the early hours of the morning, at dusk or just before nightfall. It has been proven that attacking in low-light conditions results in success, since enemy gunners in rear positions, or those positioned to provide flanking fire, lack visibility. In addition, the Soviet soldier seems to be less supervised which makes it easier for us to attack his bunkers. Mud and snow make the attack more difficult, which slows the progress of our PzGren. Armoured personnel carriers, used responsibly and according to their capabilities, are a valuable help.

At night a wedge-shape attack formation, with a strong leading element, has proven to be very effective. Shooting from all guns (machine guns, machine pistols and rifles) to the front and sides, combined with loud shouts of 'Hurrah' from our troops seriously unnerves the enemy. Those armoured carriers mounting heavy weapons, grenade launchers [mortars] or anti-tank weapons were invaluable.

The strength of our defence, particularly by a relatively small number of troops, lies not only in how various weapons are used, but the way in which all local reserves are deployed. For example: a Soviet regiment (usually 300 men, including artillery observers and pioneers), which had broken through at night, was annihilated within

An SdKfz 10/5 carefully positioned behind a row of trees to support advancing PzGren. The 2cm FlaK gun was very effective in this role, since it could be loaded with high-explosive or armour-piercing rounds and had a high rate of fire.

An SdKfz 251/7 *Panzer-Pionierwagen* (PzPiWg – armoured engineers carrier) in service with the *Panzer-Pionier-Kompanie* (PzPiKp - armoured engineer company) of 4.PzDiv. The vehicle is carrying thick planks of wood in place of the *Übergangsschienen* (bridging sections).

an hour by 30 of our troops (three groups) which had attacked from different sides. We counted 145 enemy dead, and 80 prisoners were taken.

A captured Red Army captain being interrogated stated: 'If only we had known that you were so weak.'

In addition to the undeniable usefulness of the armoured personnel carrier, the report clearly shows that the weakened German units were no longer capable of launching a major offensive. Instead, they were forced to defend their lines and, where possible or necessary, counterattack to regain lost territory.

PzGrenWg – Increased Firepower

From the time when production of the SdKfz 251 medium armoured personnel carrier – later *mittlere Schützenpanzerwagen* (m SPW – medium armoured infantry carrier) – commenced, so did the design and development of a number of variants to fulfill specific combat duties.

As the war expanded and new battlefronts opened, combat experience dictated that further variants would be required and military planners issued corresponding specifications and by 1945, the number of variants to enter service had increased to 23. In 1943, some 25 percent of the SdKfz 251 delivered were the basic SdKfz 251/1 infantry carrier; 18 percent were SdKfz 251/3, *mittlere Funkpanzerwagen* (m FuPzWg – medium armoured radio vehicle) and 20 percent were SdKfz 251/7, *mittlere Pionierpanzerwagen* (m PiPzWg – medium armoured engineer's vehicle).

Although the SdKfz 251/9, mounting a 7.5cm *Sturmkanone* (StuK – assault gun) 37 L/24 and known as the *Kanonewagen*, along with the SdKfz 251/16, *Flammpanzerwagen* (FlPzWg – armoured flamethrower vehicle), had proven to be very effective in service, military planners identified a requirement for even more firepower. Consequently, three new variants of the SdKfz 251 entered service in 1944.

SdKfz 251/17

The powerful 2cm *Flugzeugabwehrkanone* (FlaK – anti-aircraft gun) 38 was also used, very successfully, as a *Kampfwagen-Kanone* (KwK – tank gun). (The same gun had already been mounted on the SdKfz 10/4 and SdKfz 10/5 as a heavy infantry support weapon and was an integral part of PzGren units).

In 1944, military planners decided to install the 2cm FlaK 38 as a heavy machine gun in the SdKfz 251.

A *Schwebelafette* (suspended carriage) was designed and installed on a four-legged turntable-type mounting in the centre of the fighting compartment.

A company of SdKfz 251 from SS-PzDiv Wiking break cover to cross an open field. Note an 8.8cm *Raketen-Panzerbüchse* (RakPzB – rocket assisted anti-tank rifle) 54, also known as the *'Panzerschreck'* (tank fright), has been carelessly strapped on the side of the vehicle.

Right: From the SdKfz 251 Ausf D onwards, the rear panel of the *Panzeraufbau* (armour body) was altered and fitted with simplified doors.

Below: The machine gunner of an SdKfz 251/3, from the 5.SS-PzDiv Wiking, receives instruction on firing the 7.92mm *Maschinengewehr* (MG – machine gun) 42 during a training exercise.

The crew of an SdKfz 251/16 *Flammpanzerwagen* (armoured flame-thrower vehicle) were supplied with special fireproof clothing. The crew compartment also carried two 350-litre tanks containing flame fuel and a high-pressure pump powered by a small petrol engine.

In 1944, the mounting for the 7.5cm StuK 37 L/24 in the SdKfz 251/9 was significantly simplified to provide more space in the crew compartment.

The gunner sat on a seat fitted to the mounting, aiming the gun manually and using his body weight to compensate that of the 2cm FlaK 38.

Another type of suspended carriage, the *Hängelafette*, was also produced for the weapon. Although no information is known about this equipment it continues to be shown in various lists for the SdKfz 251/17 up until January 1945.

The SdKfz 251/17 replaced the SdKfz 251/10, armed with 3.7cm PaK, which was then in service with PzGrenKp.

SdKfz 251/21

By July 1944, the *Waffenamt* proposed a further m SPW version mounting heavy machine weapons.

In 1939, Waffenfabrik Mauser began design work on the 15mm *Maschinengewehr* (MG – machine gun) 151/15 to improve the hitting power of *Luftwaffe* fighter aircraft. The weapon was first fitted in the Messerschmitt Bf 109F-2, but it was soon found to be less effective than planned. It was then redesigned by Mauser as the 20mm MG 151/20 which became, from 1941, the standard armament for the Messerschmitt Bf 109F-4 and all subsequent

versions. The weapon went into mass production at Mauser and any surplus weapons were made available to the *Wehrmacht*.

Subsequently military planners envisaged using the weapon to arm an anti-aircraft version of the SdKfz 251 and ordered design work to commence immediately. The result was an assembly of three autocannons, protected by a three-sided armour gun shield, fitted on a pedestal-type mounting. A seat for the gunner was suspended from the gun frame which was traversed and elevated by a hand-operated mechanism. The weapon was muzzle heavy, but this was counterbalanced by the weight of the gunner. Some 750 rounds of ammunition were stowed in three separate large bins. The SdKfz 251/21, was commonly known as the '*Drilling*' (triple).

As Allied bombing raids increased, German aircraft production slowed, resulting in an even larger surplus of MG151/15 and MG151/20 autocannons. Military planners issued a directive for the weapon to be mounted on a truck or the 1,500kg *Sonderanhänger-Ost* (special trailer-East) two-axle trailer specially produced to be towed by a *Raupenschlepper-Ost* (RSO – fully tracked tractor-East). In the turmoil of the last days of the war, a number were mounted on railway wagons or even used static position.

Four SdKfz 251/1 armoured personnel carriers from 5.SS-PzDiv Wiking on exercise in Poland during the summer of 1944.

Above: The 14mm
Flammenwerfer (flame
thrower) had a maximum
range of 50–60m. Army
regulations stated
that the SdKfz 251/16
Flammpanzerwagen
could only be deployed in
combination with other
armoured forces.

Right: The
Flammpanzerwagen carried
sufficient flame fuel for up to
80 two-second bursts of fire.

The first 50 SdKfz 251/21 were delivered in December 1940 and mounted the MG 151/15, but apparently all other production vehicles were armed with the MG 151/20. It is difficult to determine exactly how many of each version were completed, since the *Rüststand* tables, dated 1 March 1945, show that 305 vehicles had been produced between October 1944 and 1 March 1945; whereas the number indicated for one month is, confusingly, 273.

In August 1944, orders were issued for the SdKfz 251/21 to be initially delivered to all newly established Panzer brigades, so that the type could be deployed in platoon strength as part of a PzGrenKp in accordance with KStN 1114 'a', 'b' and 'd'.

The various heavy weapons mounted on the SdKfz 251 brought about a considerable increase in the firepower for PzGren battalions, companies and platoons. In particular those mounting 15mm, 20mm *Drilling* autocannons, the 2cm FlaK 38 or the 7.5cm StuK L/24 guns, and also vehicles equipped to launch 28cm or 32cm *schwere Wurfkörper* (heavy missiles) rockets or fitted with *Flammenwerfer* (flame thrower) equipment, often enabled a *Kampfgruppe* (armoured battle group) to gain superiority on the battlefront and secure territory. But towards the end of the war, the number of armoured carriers being built was never sufficient to fully equip a new unit or to compensate for combat losses. Finally, as an almost futile attempt to halt the massed formations of Red Army tanks advancing on the Reich, military planners decided to mount an anti-tank gun on the SdKfz 251 to create a self-propelled tank destroyer.

SdKfz 251/22

In October 1944, a plan was announced to equip a number of SdKfz 251 (also the SdKfz 234 heavy armoured car) with the 7.5cm PaK 40 L/46, despite the risk of the heavy anti-tank gun overloading the carrier vehicle. This was mounted in the vehicles by means of simple steel frames. The version based on the SPW received the designation SdKfz 251/22.

Hitler was enthusiastic about this solution; he subsequently decided to halt production of the SdKfz 251/9 in favour of the new 'PaK-Wagen'. The production number is not exactly known, but it is estimated that between 120 and 200 were built.

On the organizational level, the SdKfz 251/22 replaced the SdKfz 251/9 in the PzGrenKp.

By the end of 1944, the *mittlere Mannschaftstransportwagen* (m MTW – medium personnel carrier) had finally evolved into the *Panzergrenadierwagen* (PzGrenWg) – the first armoured infantry fighting vehicle.

The distinctive shape of the *Panzerschürzen* (side armour) fitted on this *Sturmgeschütz* (StuG – assault gun) indicates that it is in service with StuGBrig 905. The SdKfz 10/5, of an unknown PzGren unit, has been fitted with standard additional armour.

Above: Field engineers working to fit a 2cm *Kampfwagenkanone* (KwK – tank gun) 30 and MG 34 in an SdKfz 251 Ausf D. The gun assembly had been salvaged from a damaged SdKfz 222 *Panzerspähwagen* (PzSpWg – armoured car).

Right: The factory-built SdKfz 251/17 was described as a 2cm *Selbstfahrlafette Flugzeugabwehrkanone-wagen* (self-propelled anti-aircraft vehicle).

Above: Here field engineers have fabricated a simple heavy bracket to mount a 2cm FlaK 38 directly on the *Panzeraufbau* (armour body) of an SdKfz 251. The weapon is fitted with a shoulder stock to make it easier for the gunner to aim.

Left: A field engineer unit has fabricated a traversing and elevating mechanism for this 2cm FlaK 38 mounted in an SdKfz 251.

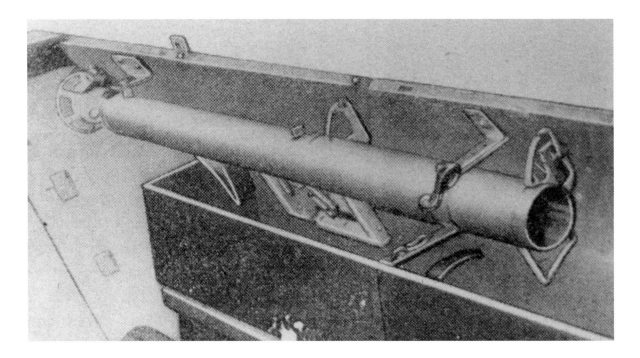

In February 1945, a *Heerestechnisches Verordnungsblatt* (HVBT – army technical bulletin) was issued to front-line workshop units for fitting brackets to carry such weapons as the 8.8cm *Raketen-Panzerbüchse* (RakPzB - rocket assisted anti-tank rifle) 54, or the *Panzerfaust* (armour fist).

Troop Conversions

The troops were very resourceful in increasing the combat value of their armoured personnel carriers. Weapons captured from the enemy, such as the Browning 0.50-inch heavy machine gun used by the US Army or those weapons captured from the Red Army, which included the 12.7mm DShK heavy machine gun and the 14.5mm *Protovo Tankovoya Rozhya Degtyaryova* (PTRD – single-shot anti-tank weapon) rifle, were often taken and mounted on German vehicles. It was also common practice for field engineers to salvage any serviceable 2cm KwK or 2cm FlaK 38 from damaged vehicles, and remount them in order to provide firepower.

The *Oberkommando des Heeres* (OKH – Army High Command) published a set of simple instructions in the *Allgemeine Heeresmitteilungen* (AHM – general army communication) on how to protect and safely carry delicate anti-tank weapons, such as the 8.8cm *Raketenpanzerbüchse* (RakPzB – rocket-propelled anti-tank rifle) 54 or RakPzB 54/1, inside an armoured personnel carrier. But for other weapons, such as the *Panzerfaust* (armoured fist) and *Panzerschreck* (tank shock) which were in fitted in long boxes, some of the bench seating in the vehicle had to be removed.

Production

Under the leadership of Albert Speer, the *Minister für Bewaffnung und Munition* (minister for armament and ammunition), the production of m SPW (SdKfz

251) progressively increased. In 1944, the minister set a target of some 700 units a month and this was almost achieved, but the number of the lighter SPW (SdKfz 250) completed was, for many reasons, never as expected. This vehicle was primarily to be issued to armoured reconnaissance units (SdKfz 250/5 and SdKfz 251/9), and as a radio/command vehicle (SdKfz 250/3).

	Production le SPW	Stock 250/8	Stock 250/9	Stock other variants
January 1944	220	0	289	2,498
February 1944	197	0	279	2,498
March 1944	103	0	258	2,570
April 1944	107	0	196	2,515
May 1944	100	0	224	2,067
June 1944	64	**	246	2,073
July 1944	130	**	219	2,057
August 1944	201	**	266	1,913
September 1944	142	**	273	2,045
October 1944	204	8	304	2,364
November 1944	28	10	380	2,334
December 1944	205	12	395	2,392
January 1945	91	8	385	2,429
February 1945	102	5	419	2,341
March 1945	76	**	**	**
April 1945	0	**	**	**
May 1945	0	**	**	**

	Production m SPW	Stock 251/9	Stock 251/16	Stock 251/17	Stock 251/21	Stock other variants
January 1944	554	303	*	*	*	3,719
February 1944	723	384	*	*	*	4,069
March 1944	848	415	*	*	*	4,913
April 1944	645	367	*	*	*	5,001
May 1944	669	367	*	*	*	5,581
June 1944	600	390	*	*	*	5,983
July 1944	568	430	*	*	*	6,169
August 1944	837	545	*	*	*	6,894
September 1944	754	569	258	53	61	4,860
October 1944	600	626	265	65	90	5,093
November 1944	521	636	274	111	138	5,243
December 1944	466	632	277	104	241	5,374
January 1945	483	582	255	110	273	5,292
February 1945	360	0	**	**	**	**
March 1945	173	0	**	**	**	**
April 1945	0	**	**	**	**	**
May 1945	0	**	**	**	**	**

* not available, partly included in other variants ** not available

From October to March, the road conditions in the east were bad. The autumn rain saw the onset of the *Rasputitsa* (mud season), which was followed by the heavy snow and deep frost of winter. When the thaw began the heavy mud returned. Only tracked and half-tracked vehicles were able to cope with these conditions.

As with the SdKfz 251, the available armament statistics for the le SPW (SdKfz 250) from 1944 onwards only show totals. Only the heavily armed variants SdKfz 250/8 (7.5cm K 51) and SdKfz 251/9 (2cm KwK 38) were shown separately.

In 1943, despite the increase in production, it was not possible to issue more than one of the four PzGrenBtl in each Panzer division with the armoured personnel carrier.

In February 1944, the senior *Panzeroffizier beim Generalstab des Heeres* (GenStbdH – tank officer at the army general staff), presented a more realistic view of the actual situation. He explained the 'impossibility' of creating a second armoured PzGrenBtl in a Panzer division, since at that time some 800 medium armoured personnel carriers were being produced each month – this number was almost achieved in 1944 – and there was a total of 32 Panzer divisions (including SS Panzer divisions): a total of 7,456 would be required to issue 233 to equip one battalion in each division. At the beginning of 1944, the actual stock of SdKfz 251 was noted as 2,221 vehicles; a clear deficit of 5,235. Total production for 1944 would not be sufficient even to cancel out the lack of vehicles. By using, as a basis, the numbers required to equip two armoured PzGrenBtl in each division, then a total of 10,368 medium armoured carriers would be needed.

However, the above calculation places a clear question mark over the official figures, contained in the *Rüststand* tables for December 1943, which show the number of SdKfz 251 held in a stock as over 4,000 vehicles. The discrepancy cannot be explained but, it is possible that the *Panzeroffizier* knowingly falsified the entries in order to emphasize his claims.

A *Waffenamt* document, dated 27 March 1945, contains a directive issued by *Oberstleutnant* Wolfgang Thomale, the liaison officer between the *Befehlshaber des Ersatzheeres* (commander-in-chief of the replacement army) and Albert Speer, explaining the ongoing problems as the end of the war approached.

Various production problems
SdKfz 251:
The breakdown of the various variants for the remaining 800 SdKfz 251 as proposed at the conference on 24 February, is in progress. Among them are a total of 50 SdKfz 251/7 and SdKfz 251/11, which will now be assembled as standard SdKfz 251/1, and without the *Einbausätze* [installation kits] which are considered to be superfluous. Production of the SdKfz 251/3 is to begin again at Weserhütte.

The radio operator of an SdKfz 251/3 *Funkpanzerwagen* (armoured radio vehicle) appears to be opearing the volume control of his *Panzer-Kopfhörer* (headset).

Below: The *Funkgerät* (FuG – radio device) 8 would be attached to a *Sternantenne* d (star antenna) for long-range communications. A 1.4m rod antenna for the *Funksprech* (FuSpr – transceiver) 'f' is mounted on the front of the vehicle.

A PzGrenRgt was authorized to be issued six 15cm sIG 33 (Sf) to form an infantry gun company. The vehicle, commonly known as the 'Grille' (cricket), was built on the chassis of a PzKpfw 38(t) and produced as two *Ausführung* (Ausf – model): Ausf H [above] was rear engined; the later Ausf M had the engine in the front.

In addition, some 200 extra medium armoured carriers can be delivered by reducing the number of half-track tractors being produced. The majority being delivered are SdKfz 251/3; the rest are SdKfz 251/21 [MG 151/20], SdKfz 251/22 [7.5cm PaK 40] and SdKfz 251/1.
An emergency programme must be initiated to produce a minimum of 270 SdKfz 251 each month. This will require some 3,000 petrol engines, but these are yet to be procured.

Another indication of the precarious production situation is the explicit order to dismantle the installation kits from all lost SPWs and send them back to the Reich for reuse.

Organizational Changes

When implementing the PzDiv 43 structure, it was planned to equip one of the four PzGrenBtl in a division with armoured personnel carriers so that each would have a regimental staff section with two SdKfz 251 and a staff company issued with 20 of the type. The PzGrenBtl (gep) was to have a battalion staff company with six SdKfz 251, three PzGren companies each issued with seven SdKfz 251, and a heavy company with 27 medium carriers. The regiment had two self-propelled infantry gun companies, each issued with four SdKfz 251. This organizational structure shows no separate pioneer company, but each PzGrenKp was to have a PiZg in its *schwere Kompanie* (heavy company).

PzGren of 5.SS-PzDiv Wiking appear to be questioning a Polish farm worker. Note the 8.8cm *Raketen-Panzerbüchse* (RakPzB – rocket assisted anti-tank rifle) 54 has been mounted on the side of this SdKfz 251, despite its susceptibility to damage.

The 'ideal' formation of a PzDiv 43-type PzGrenBtl (if there was ever such a thing) would have had a *SturmFlaK-Kompanie* (SturmFlaK-Kp) issued with six or twelve SdKfz 10/5 self-propelled guns (2cm FlaK 30 or 38). But as shown in the table, this company was not allotted to every PzGrenBtl which, in turn, meant that the PzGrenRgt also did not show any anti-aircraft elements.

When the PzDiv 44 structure was implemented, the basic configuration of a PzGrenRgt did not fundamentally change and, once again, only one battalion (gp) was issued with armoured carriers. Among the few differences was that the number of 12cm s GrW 42 heavy mortars issued rose from 12 to 16. The SturmFlaK-Kp was totally dropped, possibly because of the inclusion of seven SdKfz 251/17 in the PzGrenKp 'c' (KStN 1114 'c'), which supported the PzGrenKp in both ground combat and anti-aircraft defence.

The PzDiv 44 structure was valid from September 1944, but was it was only completely implemented in a limited number of Panzer divisions.

The introduction of new armoured half-track variants resulted in the organizational structures for each respective PzGrenKp being adapted. A table published in July 1944 by the OKH, shows that I./PzGrenRgt 3 (3.PzDiv) had three PzGrenKp and a heavy company, and that seven SdKfz 251/17 were authorized to be issued to a standard PzGrenKp. But a hand-written correction on one of the original documents indicates that a number of these highly valued vehicles were replaced by standard SdKfz 251/1, possibly due to the omnipresent delivery problems.

All regimental armoured pioneer elements were concentrated in one PzPiKp (gp), having, among other subunits, one PzGren Flamm-Zug (gp), SdKfz 251/16) and a PzGrenPiZg (gp) (SdKfz 251/5 and SdKfz 251/7).

The divisional armoured engineer battalion (PzPiBtl 39) in 3.PzDiv had an additional PzPiKp (gp), issued with SdKfz 250/11 (2.8cm s PzB 41), as well as SdKfz 251/2 (8cm GrW 34) and SdKfz 251/16.

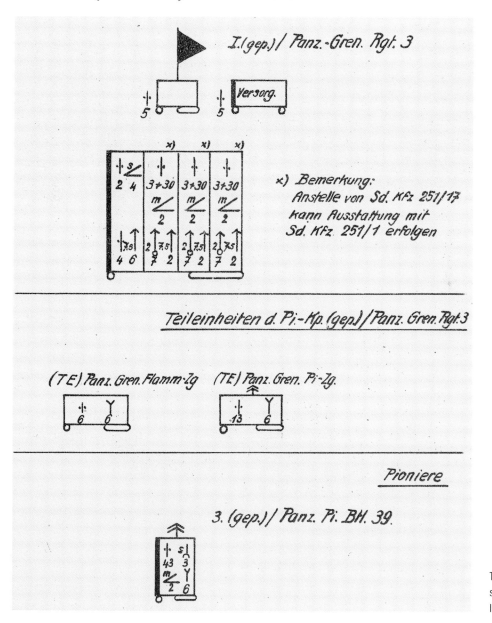

The organizational structure of I./PzGrenRgt 3 in 1944.

An SdKfz 251/3
Funkpanzerwagen in
service with the regimental
staff of 5.SS-PzDiv Wiking
to allow communication
between troops on the
battlefront and command
echelons.

Armoured Battle Groups

At the beginning of 1944, the lack of armoured vehicles became noticeable within all German units, especially on the Eastern Front.

On 1 January 1944, 3.PzDiv issued a status report which noted that it had ten PzKpfw IV (target 93) and 44 armoured personnel carrier or reconnaissance vehicles (target 264) operational.

The commander, *Oberst* Rudolf Lang also wrote:

> The mechanical condition of our motor vehicles continues to deteriorate further and we have not received any of the requested replacements. The lack of transport vehicles and cars for commanders, at all levels, inhibits our operations. In our Grenadier regiments, it is only possible to improvise a medium-sized battalion for combat duties. The artillery can only carry 30 percent of its ammunition, and an entire battery had to be decommissioned due to the lack of tractors.
>
> For the same reason, we are severely restricted as to how and where we can deploy our heavy PaK [7.5cm/7.62cm anti-tank guns]. As a result, we rejected an offer of more heavy anti-tank guns from the army.

A month later, Lang sent another report listing further problems. The number of his troops falling sick had risen significantly due to the weather conditions; frost and rain soaked clothing and the wet mud destroyed felt boots. He also complained about inadequate delousing facilities and the general lack of basic hygiene. But Lang did note that the overall morale of his troops was surprisingly good due to many successful combat operations in the past month.

Lang continued his report:

Special difficulties

A serious shortage of PzGren (trench strengths are desperately low) leads to all existing numerically weak companies being constantly overburdened. The replacement soldiers are unable to cope with this increased physical exertion, and often fall back. The vehicle situation has deteriorated further. At present, spare parts have to be collected by the division from depots, often over 1,000km distant, which results in a delay of up to six weeks. A substantial number of the vehicles, especially the mechanically complicated armoured vehicles, lie immobile and useless at the repair facilities awaiting spare parts. There is a danger that they will be lost, due to a lack of towing vehicles, if (or when) we have to make a retreat. Currently, two heavy batteries in our artillery are immobile due to having no suitable tractors. Finally, the poor condition of Russian roads is often the main cause of numerous vehicle breakdowns.

Deployment of *Panzerpioniere* [armoured engineers] on the battlefield is currently not possible due to a shortage of armoured carriers. This also affects the PzGrenRgt which without carriers is unable to follow up any successful tank assault; as a consequence, it

An SdKfz 10/5 mounting a 2cm FlaK 38 enters a bridge, built by German pioneers, over a river on the Kursk salient. Note the ammunition boxes on the side of the vehicle: more was carried in the *Sonderanhänger* (SdAnh – special purpose trailer) 51.

is impossible for our PzGren to exploit any success by flushing out any remaining enemy infantry to take and hold the territory gained.

The desperate shortage of radio and telephone equipment makes the transmission of orders, between commanders and those in the field considerably more difficult.

Finally, we find the shortage of soap, especially shaving soap (last allocation received in October), particularly intolerable.

Panzergrenadier-Kompanie c (gp) (KStN 1114c)
Theoretical structure as of 1 November 1943

Grp Führer	Pz* Zers-Trp	1.* Zug	2.* Zug	3.* Zug	4.* (schwerer) Zug	Kfz Inst-Zug	Gefechts-Tross	Gepäck-Tross
SdKfz 251/3	SdKfz 251/17 (2 cm)	SdKfz 251/17 (2 cm)	SdKfz 251/17 (2 cm)	SdKfz 251/17 (2 cm)	(symbol)	Lkw 3 t	le gl Pkw	Lkw 3 t
SdKfz 251/3		SdKfz 251/1	SdKfz 251/1	SdKfz 251/1	SdKfz 251/3	Lkw 3 t	Lkw 3 t	
(symbol)		SdKfz 251/1	SdKfz 251/1	SdKfz 251/1	SdKfz 251/17	SdKfz 7	Lkw 3 t	
(symbol)		SdKfz 251/1	SdKfz 251/1	SdKfz 251/1	SdKfz 251/17		Lkw 3 t	
(symbol)					SdKfz 251/2 (8 cm)			
(symbol)					SdKfz 251/2 (8 cm)			
					SdKfz 251/9 (7.5 cm)			
					SdKfz 251/9 (7.5 cm)			

* SdKfz 251/17 was not available in Nov 1943. Vehicle was substituted by SdKfz 251/1 or /10. When the *FlaK-Wagen* were introduced in 1944, they were introduced into the designated posts upon availability. *Panzer-Zerstör-Trupp* was armed with three RakPzB 54 (*Panzerschreck*).

A theoretical organizational structure of PzGrenKp 'c' (gp).

It is something of a mystery how 3.PzDiv could make any 'successful' tank assaults, as in March 1944 the division reported that it had just one operational tank: the authorized battalion of PzKpfw V Panther had not materialized. Their complete inventory of armoured personnel carriers, armoured cars and artillery observer tanks came to a combined total of 22.

Damaged or abandoned tanks that could not be recovered due to the lack of tractors were usually blown up by their crews or field engineers. Those tanks lost could not be replaced due to the supply situation.

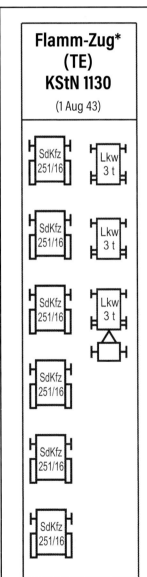

Flamm-Zug* (TE)
KStN 1130
(1 Aug 43)

SdKfz 251/16	Lkw 3 t
SdKfz 251/16	Lkw 3 t
SdKfz 251/16	Lkw 3 t
SdKfz 251/16	
SdKfz 251/16	
SdKfz 251/16	

*Flame-thrower platoon (subunit) as attached to PzGrenRgt staff or staff company, or to PzPiKp (Ausf B) engineer co.

12 cm GrWrf-Zug* (TE) KStN 1126 (1 Nov 44)			
Zug-Trupp	1. Gruppe	2. Gruppe	Mun Staffel**
	SdKfz 251/1 — 12	SdKfz 251/1 — 12	SdKfz 251/1 Wurfrahmen
	SdKfz 251/1 — 12	SdKfz 251/1 — 12	SdKfz 251/1 Wurfrahmen
SdKfz 251/1			Lkw 3 t
			Lkw 3 t

* Heavy grenade launcher platoon (subunit) as attached to heavy company of PzGrenBtl
** Ammunition section included two SdKfz 251 with *Wurfrahmen* (frame) for six *schwere Wurfkörper* (heavy rockets).

Both the *Flammenwerfer-Zug* (flame-thrower platoon) and the 12cm *Granatwerfer-Zug* (GrWZg – grenade launcher [mortar] platoon) were versatile *Teileinheiten* (TE – subunits).

Under these circumstances, any thought of completely converting the PzGren units to medium armoured personnel carriers was simply a dream.

As an expedient, a decision was made to combine those elements of a Panzer division that were still able to fight into *gepanzerte Kampfgruppen* (armoured battle groups). These were to be formed by assembling all available tanks, self-propelled artillery, reconnaissance armoured cars, PzGren and armoured engineers. Only an experienced officer was to command each of these versatile and highly mobile groups. The *Kampfgruppen*, although smaller in size, corresponded in combat ability to that of an armoured division: maximum mobility and firepower.

The decision, although born from necessity, had a remarkable side effect. A close bond was formed between all armoured forces, including those in tanks and personnel carriers, which often played to their advantage in battle. Often when trapped in a hopeless situation, which were frequent due to the poor supply situation, their camaraderie enabled them to achieve surprising success.

Combat strength reports submitted at the beginning of 1944 indicate that the situation in 13.PzDiv was comparable to that of 3.PzDiv.

A report was delivered by the commander of 13.PzDiv describing his experience with *gepanzerte Kampfgruppen* (armoured battle groups):

Far left: A PzGren Trupp (squad) take cover behind a Soviet T-34 tank. All are wearing *Winter-Wendeuniform* (reversible winter uniform), which was white on one side and had *Splittertarnmuster* (splinter-pattern camouflage) on the other.

Below: The VW Typ 166 *Schwimmwagen* (swimming vehicle), was designed to replace the large number of heavy motorcycle combinations in service with German forces, as it was more versatile and cheaper to produce.

A PzGren fires at a 'target' for the benefit of a photographer from a propaganda unit. The *Maschinenpistole* (MP – machine pistol) 40 – the famous Schmeisser – was designed for close combat and was certainly not a long-range weapon.

The ideal composition of a *gepanzerter Kampfgruppe*:

The single elements in the force do not belong to any integrally formed unit. The composition of the armoured force in many past battles resulted mainly from the following:

One PzGrenBtl with armoured personnel carriers and elements of the PzAufklAbt, equipped with 15 to 25 different variants.

One Panzer company, at least a battalion, with an average of ten to 15 PzKpfw III and PzKpfw IV.

In some instances, a StuG battalion with four to six assault guns.

One PzJgKp (Sfl), (7.5cm or 8.8cm) with four to ten guns.

One 2cm FlaK battery (Sfl) with three to five halftracks.

One artillery battalion (Sfl), with a combined strength of ten *Hummel* [bumble bee] and *Wespe* [wasp] guns.

This composition proved to be workable for the planned counterattack. We did endeavour to use, where possible, any armoured vehicle that was serviceable.

Tasks

The armoured battle group is primarily used as an intervention force to re-establish our front-line position or to establish connection with cut-off units. Wherever possible, the group must be deployed close behind those areas of the frontline being threatened. Any lengthy operations will inevitably lead to mechanical failures, especially with the tracked vehicles. The armoured battle group is not a Panzer division, and cannot be used for long-range operations. It must be held close-by, limited in the number of objectives it is deployed against and it must be ensured that any success achieved on the battlefront can be maintained. For this purpose, infantry must be kept ready to occupy the territory gained.

Difficulties

Since the single elements in a battle group do not belong to one specific unit, the first action must be to create a cohesive force. In addition to the allocation of army troops (StuG and heavy tank destroyers), some of which were only attached during the operation, it happened that the available tanks were provided by up to three tank divisions.

Both the parts of our Panzer division and the detached elements of other units have the natural desire to return to their old units as quickly as possible after deployment. The

The top edge on each side of the *Panzeraufbau* (armour body) was fitted with a bar for the crew to attach items such as helmets, gas masks and backpacks.

Panzergrenadier-Kompanie a (gp) (fG*) (KStN 1114a)
Structure as of 1 August 1944

Grp Führer	1. Zug	2. Zug	3. (schwerer) Zug	4.** (Drilling) Zug
SdKfz 251/3	SdKfz 251/1	SdKfz 251/1		
SdKfz 251/3	SdKfz 251/1	SdKfz 251/1	SdKfz 251/3	SdKfz 251/21 3 MG151
le gl Pkw	SdKfz 251/1	SdKfz 251/1	SdKfz 251/2 8 cm	SdKfz 251/21 3 MG151
le gl Pkw	SdKfz 251/1	SdKfz 251/1	SdKfz 251/2 8 cm	SdKfz 251/21 3 MG151
			SdKfz 251/9 7.5 cm	SdKfz 251/21 3 MG151
			SdKfz 251/9 7.5 cm	SdKfz 251/21 3 MG151
				SdKfz 251/21 3 MG151

* The new *freie Gliederung* (fG) structure saw a concentration of supply services (workshop, train, etc) in a separate supply company, reducing the combat companies considerably.

** The 4.Drilling-Zug was provided with six SdKfz 251/21 armed with triple MG 151 having a calibre of either 15mm or 20mm.

Organizational structures were adapted when the SdKfz 251/21 entered service.

consequence is a rapid decline in the fighting strength of the armoured task force. These efforts must be vigorously and sharply countered.

Communication within the battle group is difficult due to the diverse equipment and the continuing lack of radios. This is why the battle group commander is unable to effectively use a Kfz 17 *Funkwagen* [radio car]. *Befehlspanzer* [command tanks] are often not available. A complicating factor is that StuG, Panzer and *Schützenpanzer* have different radios and cannot communicate with each other. The self-propelled PzJg company often has no radios at all.

Summary

Experiences gained in recent battles have shown that dynamically and boldly led armoured battle groups were successful even when faced by a superior Russian force, and were always able to defeat the enemy with relatively few losses.

This report indicates that the Panzer divisions on the frontline at the Eastern Front were hardly in a position to carry out offensive operations. Battle groups, although successfully deployed for many individual actions, were primarily suited to local and time-limited counteroffensives. Many of these resulted in the re-establishment of the frontline or clearing pockets of enemy resistance, but their actions did nothing to alter the course of the war in the East. The armoured infantry fought a losing battle, since any armoured personnel carriers lost in battle could not be replaced.

In June 1944, military planners issued an organizational structure for what they envisaged as the ideal *Kampfgruppe*. Interestingly, the tank strengths were detailed, but the number of armoured carriers was not specified.

Normandy

When Allied forces landed on the Italian mainland at Salerno on 3 September 1943, Germany was faced with fighting two formidable enemies. Although this meant that a large number of German units had to be withdrawn from the Eastern Front, relieving pressure on Soviet forces, Josef Stalin was not completely satisfied and demanded more action from his allies. His demand for a 'true' second front was answered 06:30hrs on 6 June 1944, when an Allied amphibious force (Operation *Overlord*) began landing troops and heavy equipment on the beaches of Normandy, France.

Many German units, including some Panzer divisions, were stationed in France as part of an occupation force. Others had been sent to the country for a rest, to be re-equipped and retrained; many were to receive the new PzKpfw V Panther or the PzKpfw VI Ausf B Tiger II, known as the *Königstiger* (King Tiger).

This SdKfz 251/8 *Kranken-Panzerwagen* (armoured ambulance) in service with PzRgt 7 (10.PzDiv) has been painted white and clearly marked red crosses identify it as a medical vehicle. Note the spare track links stowed in racks.

Although the landings were most certainly expected, German intelligence was unaware of the precise location due to carefully planned deception (Operation *Fortitude*) by the Allies. Consequently, German commanders expected Allied forces to come ashore at the Pas de Calais, which meant that a number of Panzer units remained scattered over a wide area from Bordeaux, on the west coast of France, to the Belgian city of Brussels. Only the few positioned in, or adjacent to, Normandy were able to react quickly.

But a critical amount of time was lost before the Panzer divisions were ordered into action; some was due to the incompetence of senior officers – *Generalfeldmarschall* Erwin Rommel had returned to Germany on 5 June – and also that Hitler, who had assumed overall command, could not be contacted: apparently, he was sleeping and not to be woken.

Due to these delays and being protected by total air superiority, Allied forces began to establish bridgeheads.

Several German divisions advancing towards the Normandy coast were halted as they came under fire from Allied warships, sailing along the beach line to provide supporting fire. Other Panzer units, kept in reserve – there was a disagreement at high command of when and where they were to be deployed – were attacked by free-roaming Allied aircraft as soon as they were spotted in their holding area or when they made any move towards the battlefront.

The PzGren battalions of these divisions suffered the same fate; their armoured vehicles were not invulnerable to artillery fire or ground-attack aircraft air or strikes. Subsequently, all movements such as driving to an assembly area in preparation for a counterattack, or to resupply a unit were only possible between dusk and dawn (exacerbated by the short summer nights) when Allied aircraft were unable to operate.

PzGren in PzBrig

In July 1944, Hitler issued a *Führer-Befehl* (leader's command) which ordered the establishment of ten *Panzer-Brigaden* (PzBrig – armoured brigades).

The PzBrig consisted of:
Staff with reconnaissance elements
PzAbt with 33 PzKpfw V Panther and 11 tank destroyer type Pz IV/70
PzGrenBtl (gp)
PzPi Btl

This new type of organization was to be formed from existing units, after the severe losses suffered by German forces on the Eastern Front, to create an armoured brigade that would be capable of counterattacking to destroy any

Although developed as a self-propelled anti-aircraft gun the SdKfz 251/21, which had a triple mounting fitted with three 1.5cm or 2cm cannons, was also deployed to great effect against ground targets. Troops called the vehicles *'Drillinge'* (triplets).

Panzergrenadier-Kompanie d (gp) (fG*) (KStN 1114d) MG 151/20 *Drilling*, structure as of 1 August 1944

Grp Führer	1. Zug	2. Zug	3. Zug
SdKfz 251/3			
SdKfz 251/3	SdKfz 251/21 3 MG151	SdKfz 251/21 3 MG151	SdKfz 251/21 3 MG151
le gl Pkw	SdKfz 251/21 3 MG151	SdKfz 251/21 3 MG151	SdKfz 251/21 3 MG151
le gl Pkw	SdKfz 251/21 3 MG151	SdKfz 251/21 3 MG151	SdKfz 251/21 3 MG151
	SdKfz 251/21 3 MG151	SdKfz 251/21 3 MG151	SdKfz 251/21 3 MG151
	SdKfz 251/21 3 MG151	SdKfz 251/21 3 MG151	SdKfz 251/21 3 MG151
	SdKfz 251/21 3 MG151	SdKfz 251/21 3 MG151	SdKfz 251/21 3 MG151

* The new *freie Gliederung* (fG) structure saw a concentration of supply services (workshop, train, etc.) in a separate supply company, reducing the combat companies considerably.

The PzGrenDiv 'd' (gp) was assembled for the newly established tank brigades. Each was equipped with 18 SdKfz 251/21.

enemy forces that had penetrated German lines. Due to its composition, the PzBrig was not intended to be deployed defensively.

The PzAbt would be in the forefront of an attack and closely followed by the PzGrenBtl whose riflemen were, initially, to fight from their vehicles. The new type of PzBrig did not have any other combat support units such as artillery or tank destroyer and in some respects was similar to a *Kampfgruppe*.

The first to be formed were PzBrig 101 to PzBrig 110, quickly followed by another four, but all were disbanded between September and November 1944 and their equipment distributed to other Panzer divisions. Only PzBrig 150, known as '*Rabenhügel*' (Raven Hill) survived and was issued with PzKpfw V Panther: a number of these were disguised to resemble US Army M10 tank destroyers to confuse Allied forces attempting to advance through the Ardennes.

After-action Reports

The December 1944 issue of the *Nachrichtenblatt der Panzertruppen* (bulletin of the armoured troops) published a number of after-action reports which, although containing limited information, do describe the firepower of the 2cm *Drilling* mounting:

The *Kettenkrad* (SdKfz 2) was designed and built by NSU-Werke at their facility in Neckarsulm. Stöwer of Stettin was also contracted to manufacture the type and by the end of the war some 8,345 had been delivered. The SdKfz 2/1 *Fernsprechwagen* (FuSprWg – telephone cable vehicle) was fitted to lay cable across the battlefront. The 350kg-capacity SdAnh 1/1 trailer was often attached.

The SdKfz 10/5 was a small vehicle with limited usable space for personal weapons and equipment. The six *Karabiner* (carbine [rifle]) 98k defensive weapons for the crew were carried in a rack mounted on each of the front mudguards and protected by sheet metal covers.

Operational experience with the SdKfz 251/21 mounting the MG 151/20 '*Drilling*':

The weapon, first deployed with newly established Panzer brigades on all fronts, has proven to be highly effective, as indicated in these notes extrapolated from letters and various reports:

The company has now overcome its early fears, and from now on we scare the 'Tommies' [British troops]. We have achieved seven kills during the first five days in action; the weapon shoots like a *Maschinengewehr* [MG – machine gun] 42 and we are very satisfied with how it performs. When the company is deployed as a unit, we do not create trifle, we create a mess.

The trust I have placed in the weapon has been fully justified and I confidently await orders for our next mission. Actually, some victory rings should have already been painted on the barrels of our guns, since we have shot down a number of enemy ground-attack aircraft.

Up to this day, the *Drilling*-armed [German troops called it the 'Triplet'] platoons have proven themselves to be extraordinarily effective. A Russian machine gun nest, some

A US infantryman examines a badly damaged SdKfz 251/17 which is armed with a 2cm FlaK 38 mounted on a *Schwlebelafette* (suspended carriage).

800m distant, was silenced after only a few bursts of fire; also two heavy machine guns were destroyed and an anti-tank gun put out of action at a shorter range. Prisoners under interrogation have often stated that a great fear gripped Russian troops when a Triplet appeared on the battlefront.

The *Generalinspekteur der Panzertruppe* added this comment.

The reports reproduced above give, on the whole, the picture of the 'Drilling' that was intended. With tactically correct use and well-considered deployment, the new weapon will prove its usefulness in all theatres of war.
Generaloberst Heinz Guderian.

In the same issue of the bulletin, the commander of an unidentified armoured personnel carrier-equipped battalion which had been deployed in the East for some time wrote:

A dashingly conducted, mounted operation always leads to a resounding success. The Russian cannot withstand a thrusting attack, even if he has enough anti-tank rifles and a few anti-tank guns at his disposal. If the attack does not succeed the first time, the enemy must then be directly engaged by small forces. The mass of the battalion will then bypass

A heavily camouflaged SdKfz 251/3 *Funkpanzerwagen* (armoured radio vehicle) of 116.PzDiv (Note the stylized greyhound emblem) passes an abandoned 3-inch Gun Motor Carriage (GMC) M10 tank destroyer during the Battle of the Bulge: 16 December 1944 to 25 January 1945.

A newly delivered SdKfz 251/1 Ausf D in service with an unknown Panzer division deployed to Normandy, France after the D-Day landings on 6 June 1944. The crew are armed with the K 98k rifle, which indicates that not all PzGren units had been issued with the *Maschinenpistole* (MP – machine pistol) 44 at the time of the invasion.

the enemy positions and attack from the flanks or from the rear. In such an approach, the battalion succeeded in knocking out 11 of 14 anti-tank guns – the remaining three were captured – and also two T-34 tanks. Our own losses were extremely low. It was particularly important that even in the face of heavy artillery fire, the battalion did not dismount, but continued ignoring any minor losses. The ratio of casualties between mounted and dismounted combat was approximately one to eight. Dismounting only came into question when we were targeted by enemy anti-tank guns. In the fight against these only one action is to be taken: drive on recklessly. Our losses due to anti-tank fire were surprisingly low. Night attacks are always successful, since the Russian can always be surprised by a correctly timed attack. His resistance is accordingly low. However, leading the units in a night attack is more difficult than usual. The commander must be with his leading element.

The office of *Generaloberst* Guderian issued a comment:

Mounted combat is, and will always remain, the only form of combat for the *Schützenpanzerwagen*.

Attack: the direct and isolated attack described above is an exception: a joint advance by tanks supported by assault guns and armoured personnel carriers should always be the aim. It is better to attack together with three to four tanks to fight enemy anti-tank guns than to fight alone with an armoured infantry battalion. If this battalion has to attack without tank support, then thorough preparation – including reconnaissance of the battlefront – is paramount. A direct attack should only take place when surprise is achievable; all other types of combat are forbidden because of the high losses to be expected.

The old maxim: 'Attack is the best form of defence' also applies to the combat between armoured carriers and anti-tank rifles. The slightest hesitation or even coming to a halt, gives the enemy gunners the opportunity to fire a well-aimed shot and decide the battle in its favour. An armoured carrier-equipped unit firing from all weapons will always have success on its side by daringly driving straight ahead.

As a result of enemy air superiority, the importance of a night attack has been recognized and is becoming increasingly important. Of all the armoured formations, the carrier-equipped battalion is most suited to attack independently at night. It is therefore the duty of the leaders to train their troops thoroughly in this way of fighting – especially mounted in armoured carriers – at every available opportunity.

The available reports prove the value of the *Schützenpanzerwagen*, especially the variants equipped with heavy weapons. The General Staff of the *Wehrmacht* issued an appraisal of the *Kanonenwagen* (SdKfz 251/9) and the *Granatwerferwagen* (SdKfz 251/2) in combat:

The rear of the *Panzeraufbau* (armour body) for the SdKfz 251 Ausf D was redesigned to increase internal space and also to simplify production.

Above: From 1944, it became standard practice to paint all types of ambulance in German service white and clearly mark them with prominent red crosses.

Right: An SdKfz 251/7 *Pionier-Panzerwagen* (PiPzWg – armoured engineer carrier) in service with 12.SS-PzDiv Hitlerjugend. The vehicle is carrying two *Übergangsschienen* (bridging sections).

Above: The gunner of an SdKfz 250/1 fires on a position held by British forces after they had landed at Arnhem as part of Operation *Market Garden* on 17 September 1944. Note the canopy of an Allied supply parachute in the background.

Left: The complex *Schwebelafette* (suspended carriage) mounting of a 2cm KwK 38 in a SdKfz 251/17.

Men of an unknown SS-PzDiv parade for an oath-taking ceremony to declare their allegiance to the Führer and the Fatherland.

The heavy weapons of the PzGren (*Kanonen-Zug* and *Granatwerfer-Zug*):

The SdKfz 251/9 platoon and SdKfz 251/2 platoon are the mobile 'hammers' used by the battalion commander that are to be deployed as one force under the direct leadership of the commander of the heavy company. Both platoons have the task of giving the decisive turn to the battle by concentrating their fire against the selected target.

The SdKfz 251/9 platoon use the low-trajectory weapon to hit pin-point targets, whereas the SdKfz 251 grenade launcher [mortar] platoon is used to destroy dug-in infantry. Only impassable terrain will affect the combat deployment of both types. Often the gun platoon is unable to fight, whereas the grenade launcher [mortar] can dismount the weapon to engage the enemy.

Common tasks:
    Eliminate enemy anti-tank defences
    Be the spearhead of any attack
    Wipe out any pockets of resistance

Eliminate observation posts, bunkers and heavy weapons

Halt enemy assaults or counterattacks

Both platoons fight by using:

Surprise

Sudden ambush-style opening of fire

High mobility

High accuracy

Rapid and sustained fire

High fragmentation [shrapnel] ammunition

Although the NSU *Kettenkrad* (SdKfz 2) could climb a 24-degree incline and had excellent off-road performance, it had to be driven with some caution. The vehicle had a high centre of gravity which could cause it to tip over without any warning.

Above: The Battle of the Bulge: A stretcher party passes a well-camouflaged SdKfz 251/1 after German forces had launched their counteroffensive in the Ardennes on 16 December 1944.

Right: The SdKfz 251/9 *Kanonenwagen* was a welcome reinforcement of the PzGren companies. Note the trooper using *Scherenfernrohr* (Sf – scissor's sight) to observe the target.

A prerequisite for the successful deployment of both platoons is a clearly defined mission plan that assigns targets to each platoon as precisely as possible. The plan must take into account the characteristics of the enemy positions, then select which weapon (and ammunition type) is to be used against individual targets.

The gun platoon has also to be ready to attack any target as a battle develops. In contrast, the grenade launcher platoon must, in the first instance, search for enemy observation posts and firing positions and eliminate them with carefully aimed fire.

Both platoons are considered to be a unified combat unit, so joint deployment is mandatory.

The fire from our heavy weapons creates the wedge for our PzGrenKp, in a spearhead formation, to attack enemy front-line positions. All other units deployed for the operation will follow in support.

The positioning of heavy platoons as far forward as possible allows immediate support without any time-consuming changes. This also has the extra benefit of preventing the enemy from launching a counterattack. The all-terrain capability of the armoured personnel carrier allows the attack to be accompanied by supporting forces.

In a defensive situation, the platoons must be grouped together and only be moved into firing positions on the direct orders of the division commander.

The use of both platoons without sufficient reconnaissance is prohibited. The grenade launcher [mortar] platoon is never to be used directly in the frontline.

Three SdKfz 251/1 armoured personnel carriers loaded on a railway wagon ready for delivery to the battlefront. All have been secured according to regulations with ropes and chocks.

The gun platoon must not be used as a leading platoon, for independent reconnaissance or security duties. Finally, it is prohibited for it be deployed on the frontline as a tank destroyer, an escort tank or assault gun.

Final Battles

In 1945, due to the catastrophic situation on all fronts and the effect Allied bombing was having on the production of military equipment, military planners decided that the distribution of the infantry fighting vehicles should be reorganized.

Some interesting details can be found in a memorandum produced by Guderian:

The 15cm *schwerer Infanfanteriegeschütz 33/1 auf Geschützwagen 38(t)*, (s IG a GW – heavy infantry gun on an armoured vehicle) gave the PzGrenDiv the firepower to operate successfully. The rear-engined [here] was designated SdKfz 138 Ausf H; on the SdKfz 138 Ausf M the engine was positioned in the front. Both models were known to the troops as the *'Grille'* (cricket).

Situation:

Due to Allied bombing raids, the production of armoured carriers has slumped considerably since September last year. Although the planned output of 850 SdKfz 251 was actually achieved in August 1944, delivery of the type dropped to only 414 in November. Our average monthly losses during the past year amounted to 444 each month.

Although production figures are currently rising, further bombing raids may again lead to a reduction in output. This will seriously jeopardize any attempt at maintaining the vehicle stock held by those units equipped with the SdKfz 251.

Retrospect:

In the course of the war, those units equipped with armoured carriers, PzGren battalions

The SdKfz 2 *Kettenkrad* had a top speed of 70kph which made it a useful vehicle for liaison duties. Here an officer is about to deliver orders to the commander of a PzKpfw V Panther *Befehlswagen* (PzBefWg – command tank).

Cooperation between tanks and armoured infantry resulted in many successes on the battlefield. The commander of a PzKpfw V Panther in service with 8./SS-PzRgt 5 confers with the crew of an SdKfz 251/3 *Funkpanzerwagen* (armoured radio vehicle).

and PzAufkl battalions, achieved amazing successes. It seems that the original armoured tractor [SdKfz 251] was used less as an armoured personnel carrier, but actually more as an armoured infantry fighting vehicle. A light but high-quality combat vehicle, the SdKfz 250, had emerged. There is sufficient evidence to conclude that attacks by numerous armoured carriers, driven at speed and directly at enemy anti-tank guns and infantry positions, brought great success with only minor losses. Another important factor is the riflemen having the ability to dismount for close-quarters combat where required.

Conclusion:

The realization of the value of the armoured personnel carrier as a combat vehicle should preclude it being used as an armoured transport vehicle; especially in view of the current production situation. What the tank means to the Panzer man, the armoured carrier means to the PzGren vehicle or PzAufkl: it is his very own combat vehicle.

Requirement:

As principles for future planning and distribution of armoured carrier production, I therefore consider it imperative:

A). Priority is to maintain the numbers in those units and formations that actually use the
    armoured personnel carrier as a combat vehicle and not as an armoured transport

vehicle. This only applies to armoured infantry and armoured reconnaissance units.

B). The preservation of the mobility for the leaders of armoured units, including PzDiv commanders and those of the PzArtRgt.

C). The preservation of the engineer platoons in PzKpfw VI Tiger, PzKpfw V Panther and PzKpfw IV battalions.

D). The preservation of the armoured engineer companies.

E). Armoured ambulances, in accordance to current target numbers.

All special allocations to those troops and staffs that cannot provide proper maintenance and repair facilities must be discontinued. These include, among others, *Volks-Artillerie-Korps*, *Heeres-Pionier Brigaden*, and *Armee-Werfer-Brigaden*.

In conclusion, it should be said that all the successes in this war were only achieved where the old principle was followed: *Nicht kleckern – klotzen*, [Do not waste it – make it count].

This demand seems understandable in view of the situation. The existing armoured carriers were only to be assigned to units where they were to be used for combat and not as armoured transport vehicles.

An SdKfz 251/16 *Flammpanzerwagen* (the equipment is covered with a tarpaulin) ploughs through the slush and mud of the after-winter *Rasputitsa* (mud season). The 7.5cm PaK 40 is being towed by a *Maultier* (mule) half-track truck.

The German army was forced onto the defensive on all fronts: even bold efforts – such as the Ardennes offensive in the West and the *Plattensee-Offensive* (Lake Balaton Offensive) in the East – could not change the dire situation faced by embattled German forces. The Red Army broke through the Vistula line and a seemingly endless mass of enemy tanks and rapidly broke through the defensive fortifications of the Oder line.

In this hopeless situation, the OKW tried everything to strengthen its anti-tank defences. Plans to unite the PzDiv and PzGrenDiv into a single division could not be implemented.

A complete Flamm-Panzerwagen Teileinheit (sub-unit) equipped with SdKfz 251/16. Note each has a single-digit tactical number and that the flame equipment has been covered with tarpaulins.

Epilogue

The concept of the *Schützenpanzerwagen* (armoured personnel carrier), the SdKfz 251 and to a similar extent the SdKfz 250, had proven their excellence in countless battles. Where armoured personnel carriers were available in sufficient numbers, battles could be fought and won by using speed, armour protection and various types of mounted armament. Military commanders now had the ability to bring forward reinforcements, including heavy weapons, which allowed their forces to defeat a numerically superior enemy, as it did on many occasions.

This SdKfz 251/3 Ausf C burns fiercely after being hit in the fuel tank during the during the battle for the Ardennes which began on 16 December 1944.

The *Kätzchen* (kitten)

Both the light and the medium armoured personnel carriers were based on the chassis of a half-track tractor, and could hardly be called goal-oriented developments. Even the light SdKfz 10 and SdKfz 11 suffered from insufficient ground clearance and the non-driven front axle. While this problem was still bearable for artillery traction vehicles, the overall lack of off-road mobility of the armoured personnel carriers was often criticized.

At the turn of 1942/43, work began on a new fully tracked armoured vehicle to replace the SdKfz 251. A memorandum notes the development of a medium armoured personnel carrier. To maintain secrecy, the type was given the code name '*Kätzchen*' (kitten).

In a letter, dated 22 February 1943, *Oberbaurat* Dr Ing Kniepkamp (a senior staff member at the *Heereswaffenamt*) demanded an accelerated development of this vehicle, as the previous type (SdKfz 251) was only a makeshift option that had to be replaced by a 'usable' vehicle as soon as possible.

The development contract for the new type was awarded to Auto-Union. According to a letter dated 2 April 1943, Horch – a subsidiary of Auto-Union – was to fabricate an exact wooden mock-up, using working drawings, so that internal space and seating positions could be evaluated. At this time, decisive questions such as the type and construction of the running gear as well as the gearbox and engine were still open.

Initially, it was decided to develop seven test vehicles. In the conception phase, two running gears were developed. Auto-Union preferred a running gear having *Schachtellaufwerk* (interleaved/overlapping running wheels) according to the latest German design. The wheels were of solid steel design.

At the same time, consideration was given to using the complete running gear of the PzKpfw 38(t), manufactured by Böhmisch-Mährische Maschinenfabrik (BMM), for test purposes as an alternative approach. The corresponding parts were delivered to Auto-Union in August 1943.

Already in September 1943, the completion of two prototype vehicles could be reported:

Experimental vehicle No.1 with 30mm nose armour, Horch engine and *Schachtellaufwerk* running gear and torsion-bar suspension.
Experimental vehicle No.2 with 15mm frontal armour, Maybach engine and BMM running gear with leaf-spring suspension.

In November 1943, it was reported that a complete *Luchs* (lynx) chassis was to be delivered for further trials, to allow steering and gearbox to be tested for use on the *Kätzchen*. These parts were intended for an experimental vehicle No.3 fitted with interleaved squadron running gear. It is not known whether this version was even built as a prototype.

In February 1944, experimental vehicles No.1 and No.2 were sent to Kummersdorf for extensive field trials. Contemporary reports show that test

Kätzchen - provisional specification	
Engine:	Maybach HL 66 or Horch Typ 724
Transmission:	Zahnfabrik (ZF) eight speed
Steering unit:	Renk hydrostatic
Length:	5,309mm
Width:	2,640mm
Height:	1,865mm
Weight:	10,160kg (approx)
Payload:	2,540kg (approx)
Speed (maximum):	68kph
Armour protection:	30mm (front), 11mm (superstructure)

Above: Design and development of the armoured personnel carrier codenamed *Kätzchen* (kitten), began in total secrecy at Horch (a division of Auto-Union) in April 1943.

Right: The *Versuchsfahrzeug* (test vehicle) No.1 was fitted with *Schactellaufwerk* (interleaved/overlapping running wheels) and torsion-bar suspension. It was powered by a 6,754cc Maybach HL 66P petrol engine driving an eight-speed Zahnfabrik (ZF) gearbox.

Above: Test vehicle No.2 used the running gear developed by BMM for the PzKpfw 38(t), but during the first series of trials it was found that the Auto-Union-designed gear, as used on *Versuchsfahrzeug* No.1, gave significantly better cross-country mobility.

Left: Both *Kätzchen* test vehicles had the engine mounted at the rear, with a Cardan shaft delivering power to the transmission, positioned in the front of the chassis next to the driver.

vehicle No.1 was driven for 573km which included 292km off-road; test vehicle No.2 was run for 1,648km of which 1,052km was off-road.

Contemporary documents indicate that the following variants were planned:

Variants

The *Kätzchen* was primarily designed as an *mittlerer Schützenpanzerwagen* (m SPW – armoured personnel carrier). According to the original specification issued, the type was to carry 11 men – a driver and ten infantrymen – and armed with three light machine guns. The vehicle would also be fitted with standard radio equipment.

2cm FlaK 38

Military officials at the *Waffenamt* did evaluate the possibility of mounting the 2cm KwK, fitted on a *Hängelafette* (suspended carriage), in the SdKfz 251. No precise details are known, except that they had given some consideration to the development of the 2cm KwK in a twin mounting.

Allied air forces operated with impunity over the D-Day battlefront, which made it almost impossible for German mechanized units to move in daylight. Here a well-camouflaged SdKfz 251/9 *Kanonenwagen* passes through a village in Normandy, France.

7.5cm *Kanone* 51 L/24

In 1944, the 7.5cm *Kanone* (K – canon) 51 L/24 replaced the bulky and space consuming 7.5cm KwK 37 in the SdKfz 251/9. The gun mounting was redesigned and simplified so that the K 51 could be installed on any open armoured vehicle. Documentation shows that it was planned for the *Kätzchen* to be armed with this weapon.

12cm s GrW 42

According to documents dated August 1944, Horch was contracted to develop a carrier for the considerably more effective 12cm s GrW 42. The vehicle was open topped with the weapon mounted on a semi-rotatable baseplate. Notes made during weapon trials reveal that, when fired, the 12cm s GrW 42 mortar generated a short but significant recoil load of some 106,685kg.

In the final phases of the war, desperate military planners gave priority to finding a way of improving anti-tank capabilities. One attempt was simply to mount a complete (less wheels) 7.5cm PaK 40 in the medium armoured personnel carrier. The resulting vehicle was designated SdKfz 251/22.

A PzGren section positioned in a shallow ditch in the final months of the war. Most are armed with a *Karabiner* (carbine [rifle]) 98k and are supported by an MG 42 team and also a mobile 2cm FlaK 38. All are wearing *Winter-Wendeuniform* (reversible winter uniform) with the *Splittertarnmuster* (splinter-pattern camouflage) showing.

Medium Ambulance

Trials of the *Kätzchen* had shown that the chassis had remarkable performance capabilities. All the known disadvantages of the SdKfz 251 – lack of off-road mobility due to the front wheels not being driven; extremely low ground clearance; vulnerability to mines and mechanically weak running gear which required constant maintenance – would be eliminated. The performance of the SdKfz 251, such as top speed and range was clearly surpassed.

Consequently, German military planners decided that the fully tracked chassis was the ideal basis for a *mittlerer Krankenpanzerwagen* (medium armoured ambulance) and issued a development order.

The development of the *Kätzchen* follows a similar path to that required for the design, development and trials of a completely new type of tank. The testing of all components and the necessary modifications consumed a vast amount of money, time, materials and vital production capacity. The reason the programme was discontinued towards the end of 1944 has not yet been found in any of the documents which have survived World War II.

The SdKfz 251/10 armed with a 3.7cm *Panzerabwehrkanone* (PaK – anti-tank gun) was issued to the *Zug-Führer* (platoon leader) in a PzGrenKp. Although primarily an anti-tank gun, it was an effective support weapon when firing high-explosive ammunition.

10

WEAPONRY

At the beginning of the war, the troops serving in *Infanterie-Divisionen* (infantry divisions), *Gebirgsjäger-Divisionen* (mountain divisions) and Panzer divisions were all issued with light infantry weapons (pistols and rifles). Heavy infantry weapons, including machine guns, were supplied at Regiment (Rgt), *Bataillon* (Btl – battalion), *Kompanie* (Kp – company) and *Zug* (Zg – platoon) level to specific elements, including anti-tank teams and also machine-gun squads. Artillery pieces were only deployed as direct support weapons (infantry guns and grenade launchers [mortars]), but there were also anti-tank guns to defeat enemy armour and FlaK weapons to defend against air attack:

Kurzwaffen (handguns [side arms])
Langwaffen (long firearms): *Karabiner* (carbines [rifles])
Maschinenpistolen (MP – machine pistols)
Maschinenkarabiner (machine carbines [assault rifles])
Maschinengewehre (MG – machine guns)
Infanteriegeschütze (IG – infantry guns)
Granatwerfer (GrW – grenade launchers [mortars])
Panzerabwehrkanone (PaK – anti-tank guns)
Flugzeugabwehrkanone (FlaK – anti-aircraft guns)

Handguns

Georg Luger designed and patented the Parabellum-Pistole 08, a modern automatic pistol, which was manufactured by Deutsche Waffen und Munitionsfabriken (DWM). The P 08 weapon fired 9mm ammunition which made it an excellent close-combat weapon, but it lacked long-range accuracy.

The *Karabiner* (carbine [rifle]) 98k entered service in 1935, as the standard rifle for the German army. Despite the introduction of more modern semi- and fully automatic rifles it remained in front-line use until the end of the war.

Two *Skijäger* (SkiJg - ski troops) of 78.Sturmdivision (StuDiv - assault division). The trooper on the left is armed with a 7.92mm *Maschinenpistole* (MP - machine pistol) 44: Note the use of ski sticks to steady the weapon. The other is armed with a 7.92mm *Gewehr* (gun) G 43 semi-automatic rifle; also known as the Karabiner (carbine [rifle]) 43.

The weapon entered service with the *Deutsche Heer* (Imperial German Army) in 1908 and remained standard issue until 1945.

Design work for the 9mm Walther P38 automatic pistol, which was intended to replace the Luger, began in mid-1930. The first prototypes were ready for trials in 1938 and it was ordered into production in 1939, but this did not begin until mid-1940. Despite it being a complex weapon, which made it expensive to manufacture, some 1,200,000 had been produced by the end of the war. From 1957 to 1963, the P38 was produced as the standard issue pistol for the newly formed *Bundeswehr*.

Rifle

The *Karabiner* (carbine [rifle]) 98k was introduced in 1935 as the standard rifle in *Wehrmacht* service. The bolt-action weapon fired standard 7.92mm ammunition held in a five-round magazine. The 98k could be fitted with a *Gewehrgranatgerät* (rifle-grenade launcher) which German infantrymen called the *Schiessbecher* (shooting cup). For sniper fire, the rifle could be fitted with a *Zielfernrohr* (Zf – telescopic sight) 42. The rifle remained the most widely used infantry weapon in service with the *Wehrmacht* until the end of the war in 1945.

Machine Pistols

The *Maschinenpistole* (MP – machine pistol) 38 and MP40 were almost identical in appearance. Both fired the standard 9mm ammunition as used with the P08 and P38 pistols. Originally designed as a standard weapon for crews of armoured vehicles, the weapon was also issued to company and platoon leaders. The MP was a compact but formidable weapon, having a rate of fire of 500 rounds per minute (rpm) and a maximum effective range of 200m.

Machine Carbines

In 1943, the *Gewehr* 43 (G 43) – also known as the *Karabiner* 43 – was the first successful attempt at providing the fighting soldier with an automatic rifle. It fired standard 7.92mm ammunition and had a projected rate of fire of 30rpm and was considerably more powerful than a 98k. Also, it was fitted with a detachable ten-round magazine, making it simpler and quicker to use in combat.

At the end of 1943, the G 43 was replaced by the revolutionary *Sturmgewehr* (StG – assault rifle), also known as MP 43 or MP44. The automatic gun, which had an effective range of 400m, fired 7.92mm ammunition, but with a shorter cartridge case, which allowed a much larger magazine, containing 30 rounds, to be fitted. The weapon was assembled from pressed-steel parts, not only to simplify production, but also to reduce manufacturing costs.

Machine Guns

Firing trials of a *Einheits-Maschinengewehr* (universal machine gun), designed to replace World War I weapons, were initiated in 1929 and development continued until 1934. The resulting *Maschinengewehr* (MG – machine gun) 34 began to be issued to the *Wehrmacht* in 1936. It fired standard 7.92mm rifle ammunition and had an impressive rate of fire of up to 900rpm.

The Georg Luger-designed Parabellum-Pistole P 08 was widely used by the *Heer* (army), *Kriegsmarine* (navy) and also the *Luftwaffe* (air force) in World War II. The soldier on the right is firing what was called the *lang* (long) 'Artillery Luger', due to its having a longer barrel. This weapon could be fitted with a removable stock and a *Trommelmagazin* (drum-type magazine) containing 32 rounds of ammunition.

Above: The 7.92mm *Maschinengewehr* (MG – machine gun) 34 was the first modern general-purpose machine gun to be produced for German army. Deliveries of the weapon began in 1936 and it was supplied to all arms of the *Wehrmacht* (defence force).

Right: The *Stiel-Handgranate* (stick hand grenade) was commonly issued to all front-line units, but many German troops preferred the *Eihandgrate* (egg-shaped grenade) 39.

This versatile weapon could be used with the integral bipod as a *leichte Maschinengewehr* (le MG – light machine gun) and had an effective range of 1,500m to 2,000m, but when mounted on a *Lafette* (carriage) 34, as a *schwere Maschinengewehr* (s MG – heavy machine gun), the range increased to 3,000m. The MG 34 was also mounted on all German armoured vehicles

In 1942, the *Maschinengewehr* MG 42 was introduced as the successor to the MG 34. The weapon was assembled using pressed metal – rather than machined – components. Not only did this make it much quicker and cheaper to produce; it also virtually eliminated the problems (sensitivity to cold and dirt) endemic on earlier weapons. The MG 42 used 7.92mm ammunition and had a rate of fire up to 1,200rpm.

In action, ammunition was fed to the MG 34 either by a Metall-Dauergurt (reusable metal belt) or from a Patronentrommel (saddle drum) magazine.

Field Guns

These were supplied to infantry units to provide vital direct artillery support.

The 7.5cm *leichte Infanteriegeschütz* (le IG – light infantry gun) 18 entered service in the latter months of 1939 and was supplied to infantry gun companies. The compact weapon could be used for high or low trajectory fire at ranges of respectively, 25m and 3,550m. The le IG 18 was ideal for

attacking targets that could not be defeated by machine gunners, or when mortar fire was ineffective. The gun was easy to transport, allowing it to be positioned close to the frontline. The le IG 18 fired a standard 7.5cm high-explosive shell, but in 1942 a shaped-charge round for anti-tank defence was supplied to artillery units.

The 15cm *schwere Infanteriegeschütz* (s IG – heavy infantry gun) 33 was the heaviest weapon issued to infantry and also grenadier units. As with the light gun, the s IG 33 could be used for high or low trajectory to ranges of, respectively 50m and 4,700m. Initially only high-explosive ammunition was available, but in 1942 a shaped-charge round was introduced to defeat enemy armour. Also, in 1942 the 15cm *Stielgranate* 42, a mine-type shell with increased explosive power, became available.

Mortars

The *Granatwerfer* (GrW – grenade launcher [mortar]) was a simple and relatively lightweight high-trajectory weapon. Initially the infantry and rifle regiments were issued with two different types.

The 5cm *leichte Granatwerfer* (le GrW – light grenade launcher [mortar]) 36 was issued to infantry and rifle companies, since it weighed only 14kg, which made it easy to transport. The le GrW 36 could be fired at up to 30rpm and had a maximum range of 520m, but the 5cm ammunition was later rated as ineffective.

The 8cm *schwere Granatwerfer* (s GrW – heavy grenade launcher [mortar]) 34 became the standard weapon and was widely issued to almost every front-line unit. The s GrW 34 could be fired at the same rate as a le GrW 36, but had maximum range 1,900m and the 8cm ammunition had significantly more destructive power. But the weapon was heavier, weighing some 57kg, and had to be transported as two loads.

During the Russian campaign of 1941 and 1942, large numbers of Soviet-designed and manufactured 12cm heavy grenade launchers were captured. Since the weapon had exceptional performance it was quickly pressed into German service. Eventually, the weapon was to be replicated by German engineers and then manufactured in larger numbers.

In German service it was designated 12cm *schwere Granatwerfer* (s GrW – heavy grenade launcher [mortar]) 42 and an efficient crew could fire eight to ten rounds a minute. The s GrW 42 had a maximum range of 6,000m

Anti-tank Guns

Initially, the 3.7cm *Panzerabwehrkanone* (PaK – anti-tank gun) was introduced as a light weapon that could also be moved by its crew. The gun, when firing

Far left: The 7.5cm *leichte Infanteriegeschütz* (le IG – light infantry gun) 18 served with units at battalion level. The gun could be towed by a motor vehicle (here an SdKfz 10), but was more commonly horse drawn.

Far left below: German units at regimental level were issued with the 15cm *schwere Infanteriegeschütz* (s IG – heavy infantry gun) 33 and it was the heaviest artillery weapon used by the SchtzRgt and PzGrenRgt. The weapon was normally hauled by a motor vehicle but on many occasions, it would be attached to a team of horses.

The 8cm *Granatwerfer* (GrW – grenade launcher [mortar]) 34 was the standard German infantry mortar.

standard PzGrPatr 39 ammunition, could penetrate 35mm of armour at 100m range – sufficient to defeat the armour of those light tanks built during the inter-war years – but during the fighting in France this was found to be inadequate. However, in 1943 the 3.7cm PaK was given a new lease of life when the *Stielgranate* 41, a hollow-charge round, began to be supplied in sufficient numbers to front-line units.

The 5cm PaK 38, which entered service in 1940, gave German anti-tank units a short-lived advantage, since they now had a gun which could penetrate 65mm of armour at 100m range when firing PzGrPatr 39 ammunition. The 5cm PaK 38 weighed some 900kg, which meant that it could only be moved by a half-track tractor, a heavy truck or a team of horses. But in 1941 any advantage was lost, as better-armoured Soviet tanks were engaged on the battlefront.

In 1939, German military planners initiated the design of a more powerful anti-tank gun designated the 7.5cm PaK 40. A pre-production batch was delivered by Rheinmetall-Borsig in November 1941 followed by 44 service-standard guns in April 1942: it remained in service until 1945. But the 7.5cm PaK 40 weighed some 1,425kg – too heavy for front-line forces since could only be moved by a heavy half-track artillery tractor.

As the war continued, a variety of anti-tank weapons was developed, including the *Panzerfaust* (armour fist) and *Panzerschreck* (tank shock). Both weapons, being small and lightweight, proved to be highly effective in the hands of close-combat teams. [See *History of the Panzerjäger Volume 2*; Osprey 2020].

From the first days of the *Ostfeldzug* (eastern campaign), German troops began collecting 12cm 120-PM-38 heavy mortars abandoned by the Red Army. Those in good condition were issued to front-line units as the 12cm GrW 378(r). Its performance impressed military planners and they decided that it should be replicated by a German manufacturer. The weapon eventually entered service as the 12cm *Granatwerfer* (GrW – grenade launcher [mortar]) 42.

INDEX

ACKNOWLEDGEMENTS

As with my previous books, I have searched and gathered much original information from a number of public archives, including the Bundesarchiv/ Militärarchiv in Freiburg, Germany, and the National Archives & Records Administration, Washington, USA. Furthermore, the internet-based Project for the Digitizing of German Documents in Archives of the Russian Federation was used to a great extent.

I also want to acknowledge my appreciation to my friend Peter Müller (Historyfacts) for supplying me with much vital information and advice.

Many thanks to those individuals who have also provided assistance and access to their archives and collections of other material:

Florian von Aufseß, Peter Müller (Historyfacts), Wolfgang Zimmermann, Karlheinz Münch and Henry Hoppe.

My sincere thanks to my editor Jasper Spencer-Smith, an ever-patient gentleman, for his work on my manuscript.

Finally, to Nigel Pell for his, as always, excellent page layout.

Unless otherwise indicated, all images in this book are from the Thomas Anderson Collection.

Bibliography

Panzertruppen Volume 1 and Volume 2, Thomas Jentz, Podzun-Pallas
Panzertracts, several volumes, *Panzertracts*, Maryland, USA
Erinnerungen eines Soldaten, Heinz Guderian
Deutsche Panzerwaffe, Walther Behring